D0462371

Dance
In My
Shoes

A novel by

Lynne K Pettinger

This book is based on true events. No part of this book may be reproduced, stored in a retrieval system or transmitted by any means without the written permission of the author.

Copyright © 2013 Lynne K Pettinger
All rights reserved.
ISBN: 1491076070
ISBN 13: 9781491076071
Library of Congress Control Number: 2013913362
LCCN Imprint Name: CreateSpace Independent Publishing Platform,
North Charleston, South Carolina

Dedicated to The Dancers

Grateful acknowledgement to my friend and
editor, Patricia Wolfe, for her superb work
I would like to thank
Linda Clarke, Naida Hriskow, Jean MacDonald,
Cathy MacLellan and Jane Thatcher
for their friendship and support

Dance In My Shoes

PART 1

CHAPTER 1

Annie trembled as she waited for Sister Theresa in the overheated Grade 1 classroom at St. Peter's Girls School. When the school bell rang, dismissing the class for the day, she was told to stay after class and wait for the nun. She wondered what she had done to upset the nun as she loosened the red scarf around her neck and opened the top brass button on her navy blue Red River coat that she loved.

Sister Theresa came into the classroom holding a hardwood ruler. She walked toward Annie and folded her arms under the starched bib of her habit.

Annie's heart was pounding like a drum against her six-year-old chest as she stared down at the nun's long, skinny feet laced tightly in shiny black oxfords.

"Hold out your hands," Sister Theresa demanded. Annie didn't move. The nun shook Annie by her tiny shoulders and again demanded she hold out her hands. Annie held her small, shaking hands before the angry nun.

"Take off the mittens!" the Sister yelled.

Annie pulled off the red and navy blue striped mittens that her mother had knit and placed them together on the nun's desk. Tears rolled down her cheeks and she wondered again what she had done that was so wrong.

She felt two hard slams of the ruler on each hand as Sister Theresa told her this was punishment for dropping two peels from her orange in the schoolyard at morning recess.

"Go home," she said. "Don't ever let this happen again or the next time punishment will be more severe."

Annie reached for her mittens and put them on, feeling the red welts starting to rise on her palms and the sharp tingling in her fingers. She left the heat of the school and started the long walk home. The wind was blowing hard, the snow was piling up and it was getting dark. She was feeling a little frightened. Twenty minutes later she reached her home and stepped into the vestibule. She kicked the snow off her boots, hung her coat, hat and mittens on the hook and placed her snow boots side by side. She entered the cozy, warm kitchen as her mother, Rose, reached for her and gave her a hug.

"How was your day, Annie? I was getting a little worried about you. You are never late getting home. I was just about to call your father. Did something happen at school to keep you late?"

Annie was quiet as she held out her red hands to her mother.

"Who did this to you?" Rose asked gently as she held Annie's tiny hands in her own. The warmth of her mother's hands made Annie feel safe.

"Was it Sister Theresa?"

The tears Annie tried so hard to hold back tumbled down.

"Don't worry, my little Annie. Don't worry," her mother said as her own tears started to surface. She brushed them away and told Annie to go wash up for dinner. "Your father will be home soon."

Annie heard her father's car pull into the driveway. She looked out the window as he was closing the car door holding his overcoat over his arm and his briefcase in his hand. He looked up and saw Annie in the window and smiled as he waved to her.

Annie thought her father was the smartest and best-looking man in the entire world. He was as tall as a giant, in her eyes, dark and handsome with a beautiful smile. Everyone liked him, especially the ladies at church, and sometimes he even came to her school on business although she could never figure out why the nuns would ever need a lawyer. He would always visit with Sister Theresa. Annie often wondered that if Sister Theresa liked her father so much why she wasn't nicer to her.

She ran to open the door for him. He bent down and kissed her on the cheek as her mother took his coat and he hugged her. "Dinner will be ready as soon as you get out of that suit and change into something more comfortable." He laughed and said he would only be a few minutes.

The family took their places at the dinner table and Kate, Annie's older sister by four years, said grace.

Halfway through dinner, Timothy, Annie's eight-year-old brother sitting next to her, fell off his chair. Annie reached over and helped him back onto his seat. He had been doing this for the past several weeks and was also stumbling and falling when he walked. No one talked about it but Annie knew by the worried look on her mother's face that something was wrong.

As she helped her brother up he noticed her red hands and asked what happened.

She told him Sister Theresa strapped her with a hardwood ruler for dropping two orange peels in the playground. "The bell rang, ending recess, and when I ran to the school door they must have dropped out of my hand," Annie explained.

"That was really stupid of that old nun," said Timothy. "You didn't mean to do it. What a mean old bag."

Their father almost choked on his food. "Sister Theresa is not stupid nor is she an old bag. You don't talk that way about a nun," he scolded.

Kate chimed in with her two cents and said she agreed with Timothy. "It was an accident. Annie wouldn't do that on purpose and Sister Theresa should know that."

Before another word could be spoken, Rose said it was time to clear the table and get ready to say the rosary. They gathered in the living room on their knees to begin this nightly ritual. Timothy knelt next to Annie and leaned on her for support as she made the sign of the cross and began the Sorrowful Mysteries. This took a long thirty minutes, too long as far as Annie was concerned and she had homework to do.

When the rosary was finished, Annie helped Timothy to his feet and led him to the dining room to start their homework. Rose went into the kitchen to tidy up as she did every night after prayers, and soon her father would leave the house again for several hours. She wondered where he went and guessed that he went back to work. He was a very busy, popular lawyer and he probably had lots and lots of work to do. She would never be so bold as to ask where he went but that didn't stop her from wondering.

CHAPTER 2

"Wake up, Annie. It's time to get ready for school. The snow is still falling. You will have to leave earlier so you won't be late getting to school."

Annie leapt out of bed and dressed quickly. The last thing she wanted was to be late for school and cause more trouble with Sister Theresa. The nun would probably strap her again if she was late.

She could hear Kate already at the breakfast table but Timothy wasn't going to school today because he wasn't feeling well. "Probably getting a cold," Annie thought.

After breakfast she pulled on her white winter boots with the white rabbit trim around the laces, reached up and hugged her mother goodbye. "I'll try to be extra good and careful today, Mom, and not make Sister Theresa mad at me. I don't want the ruler ever again."

Her mother kissed her and said, "You will never have to worry about the ruler again, Annie. I promise you that."

Sister Theresa was waiting outside the classroom door as the children lined up and got ready to file into the room. She was twisting the long rosary beads that hung from a belt at her waist along with a very large crucifix that almost touched the floor. She looked at Annie but didn't smile. On her command everyone entered. Annie passed by the nun, took her seat in the first row and wondered what the day would bring. Nothing like yesterday, she hoped.

The day passed slowly and her mind wandered as she looked out the window at the falling snowflakes, wondering what was wrong with Timothy and where her father went at night. The loud crack of the ruler bounced off Annie's desk and she looked up at the nun peering down at her. "Pay attention and stop daydreaming," Sister Theresa said.

Annie kept looking at the schoolroom clock on the front wall and thought the day would never end, but the three o'clock bell finally rang. Sister Margaret, the principal, came to the door and summoned Sister Theresa to her office. Everyone was dismissed from class except Annie, who was told to wait. "Now what did I do?" she wondered.

Sister Theresa followed the principal into her office where Rose was standing in front of her desk.

"Please have a seat, Mrs. O'Brien, and we can discuss the discipline imposed on Annie yesterday by Sister Theresa."

"No, thank you, what I have to say won't take long."

She looked at Sister Theresa for a minute and saw how pretty she was. She was tall and slim with piercing blue eyes but she had a hard look on her face. Her arms were folded across her chest. Rose remembered her from their high school days. She was a couple of years ahead of her and after graduation had gone to St. Xavier University to study teaching. Rose did not know her at all but she did recall how shocked everyone was when, after receiving her teaching degree, she entered the convent.

She didn't seem too pleased to see Rose.

So, this was the mighty Rose O'Brien, the nun thought. Well, she certainly wasn't what she had imagined. She was very petite, or perhaps the black mink coat with matching pillbox hat made her look smaller. Her shoulder-length dark red hair was cut in a fashionable pageboy bob. Overall, she was much prettier than expected. She could see the resemblance in Annie.

Rose calmly turned to the nun. "Yesterday you punished my daughter by hitting her with a hardwood ruler, which left red welts on her hands. Be warned, if you ever raise your voice or hand toward my daughter again, I will pull her out of this school and transfer her to the Ferndale School for Girls. That's all I have to say."

"You can't do that," was the nun's reply as her anger was starting to show. "John would never allow that to happen. Ferndale is a Protestant school and that would never be tolerated. You may think that Annie is perfect but she isn't. She needs discipline and manners and Annie doesn't seem to get much at home, otherwise she wouldn't have thrown orange peels in the school yard."

Rose picked up her red leather handbag and, as she pulled on the matching leather gloves, she turned and said very quietly, "When speaking of my husband, you show your lack of manners and respect by not referring to him as Mr. O'Brien."

The nun was aghast but before she could say another word Sister Margaret stepped in and said, "I'm sorry this happened, Mrs. O'Brien, but we do have our rules."

Rose stopped, turned and looked at the principal. "I meant what I said. Mark my words, no one is to ever touch my daughter again."

Rose opened the classroom door. "Come along, Annie. It's time to go home."

Annie reached for her mother's hand and they left the school together. Annie didn't know what happened in the principal's office and was sure she would never find out but she knew there would be no more trouble with Sister Theresa.

CHAPTER 3

Timothy wasn't getting any better. He was now having trouble breathing and more difficulty walking and keeping his balance. Dr. White, the family doctor, said he couldn't help Timothy and suggested he be taken to the Children's Hospital in Montreal for further testing. He would make all the arrangements if Rose was interested. She asked Dr. White to contact the hospital as soon as possible and arrangements were quickly made for them to leave in a week.

There was a lot of excitement getting ready for the trip. Annie helped Timothy pack his favorite books and stuffed toys, which their mom kept removing to make room for his clothes.

"You are going to have a great time, Timothy," Annie assured him on the way to the station. "Imagine going on a train. You have to remember everything so you can tell me all about it when you get back. The doctors in Montreal are really smart and they are going to fix you up so we can play baseball again. I will really miss you when you're gone but you'll be back soon and better than ever."

Annie stood with her father and Kate as the train pulled away from the station and gathered up speed. She kept waving until they were out of sight.

Rose called home nightly after arriving in Montreal. She answered Annie's questions about Timothy: Was he having fun and when would they be home? Toward the end of their second week, after countless tests were done on Timothy, the head paediatrician called Rose into his office and told her the bad news. Her son had been diagnosed with muscular dystrophy, a degenerative muscle disease. There was no cure for it and eventually he would be confined to a wheelchair.

In the meantime, he could be fitted with a back brace and braces for his legs, which they thought would help with his balance. That was all they could do for him.

She telephoned John with the terrible news and said they would be returning home in a few days.

It was the longest two weeks of Annie's life. She couldn't keep still as she waited at the train station for Timothy and her mother's arrival. She could hear the whistle blowing and the screeching of brakes as the train finally chugged into the station. A porter stood at the bottom of the steps and helped her mother down from the train. When Rose turned, her husband was at her side with Annie, and then Timothy appeared. He was wearing the braces and seemed to be in pain. He gave Annie a tired smile.

Annie couldn't understand why Timothy was wearing all those braces. The doctors were supposed to make him better but he didn't seem better. What had gone wrong? She wanted to cry but knew she couldn't do that. He was home and that was the most important thing.

CHAPTER 4

Three weeks after Rose and Timothy arrived home, Father O'Reilly and Father Sullivan appeared at the door on a cold, rainy Friday night. Annie wondered why they were here. She would never ask because her father would just say that it was adult business. She had heard it before and was also told that "Children should be seen but not heard. Don't ask questions that have nothing to do with you."

They must have been expected because Dad was home, which was really unusual. The children said hello to the priests and were sent to their rooms, but Annie sat at the top of the stairs where she couldn't be seen but could hear what was going on in the parlour.

Annie saw Father O'Reilly sitting up in the corner of the chester-field as though he were the Pope. He wasn't a big man but he had a big belly, which Annie noticed as he took the lemon tarts from the plate on the coffee table after Rose poured tea. Brushing the crumbs off his vest, he turned to Rose

"We haven't seen you at Mass, Rose, since returning from Montreal with the tragic news about Timothy's incurable disease. This Sunday the church is planning a special Mass for Timothy. With the prayers from the congregation and our faith in God, we believe miracles are possible. It is your duty to attend Mass with your children and husband and I expect you there this Sunday. There is another thing that has to be discussed. Timothy didn't receive his First Communion at the last ceremony because he was sick. The next ceremony is scheduled for the first of May when Annie will be receiving hers and Timothy can be part of that ceremony."

Annie slid down a step because she wasn't sure she heard correctly. What were they talking about? Timothy didn't have an incurable disease. He was going to get better.

Rose shifted in her chair and glanced up. She saw Annie at the top of the stairs with a puzzled look on her face.

The priest continued. "It has also been brought to my attention that Timothy is still falling at school despite the use of the braces. This disrupts the class and frightens the other children. Sister Theresa, whom you know, has volunteered to come to your home twice a week and teach Timothy. She will be here after class on Tuesdays and Thursdays beginning next week."

Rose didn't say a word during the conversation. John was paying close attention to his wife, wondering what she was thinking and how she was going to react to this suggestion. He was very concerned that her Irish temper would surface, which would not be pleasant.

Without another word the two priests stood up to leave.

At the door, Rose handed them their coats, hats and umbrellas. Father O'Reilly turned and reminded her to be at Mass the coming Sunday. John was praying that they would leave quickly before Rose lost her temper.

She spoke very quietly, barely a whisper. "John and the children will be there but I won't. You come into my home and tell me to have faith and to believe in miracles, that there is going to be a special Mass for my son. That is an insult to me. All the prayers, singing, lighting of candles and special Masses won't help Timothy. What kind of a

God would have an innocent child suffer so, and how dare you make plans for my son's schooling. Good night, gentlemen."

John saw the two priests to their car.

Annoyed, Father O'Reilly said, "You have to get your wife in line, take control, John. She has too much too say and I don't like what she is saying."

"I'll talk to her, Michael, but she is a hard-headed woman with a mind of her own."

When he returned to the house, Rose was picking up the teacups. He took them from her and put his arms around her.

"I know you are overwhelmed with Timothy's condition and so am I, but Father O'Reilly was just trying to help in the only way he knows."

"How is he helping, John?" she said in a raised voice. "By burning candles and having special Masses and the biggest insult — suggesting that nun come to our home and teach Timothy. Are you crazy?"

For the first time since coming home, Rose broke down and sobbed. John put his arms around her and held her tight.

"My hopes and dreams for our son will never be. I imagined him playing sports, graduating from high school, college, girlfriends and enjoying life. This is the worst thing that could happen."

"We still have him, Rose. Life can still hold joy for him. It's up to us. Let's call it a day and go to bed."

CHAPTER 5

A week after Father O'Reilly's visit a letter was hand delivered to Rose. It contained instructions for the parents of children who would be receiving their First Communion. It was to take place on Sunday, May 2, at 2:00 pm. A week before the ceremony the children were to make their First Confession, confessing all their sins and misdeeds. Rose wanted to rip up the letter, but she promised her husband that Annie and Timothy would receive their First Communion. She also promised him that Sister Theresa could come to the house and teach Timothy his lessons. At dinner that evening she read the letter to the family and the preparations and excitement began.

The first item on the list was Annie's First Communion dress. She and Rose went shopping and Annie selected a knee-length white taffeta dress with cap sleeves and a little bolero. The skirt was embroidered with satin flowers and pearls with the back having satin-covered buttons and a small bow at the waist. She didn't want a veil even though the instructions said she had to wear one. So, they compromised. Rose would make her a crown of real white roses with a small veil attached at the back. Annie was satisfied with that. White gloves, white stockings and white patent-leather shoes completed the outfit.

The special day was fast approaching and Annie and Timothy spent a lot of time learning and remembering all the prayers they would have to recite without making a mistake. Timothy didn't seem as interested in the whole affair as Annie, but he went along with her to keep her happy. There were times he did get caught up in her excitement, but he thought that for Annie it was all about her dress.

The day before the big event everyone gathered in the cathedral for the First Communion rehearsal and at this time they would be asked to recite their prayers. Father O'Reilly greeted them and said there would be forty children partaking in this glorious event, twenty girls and twenty boys. The girls were to line up on the left side of the aisle and the boys on the right. Slowly they were to proceed to the altar to receive their First Communion. After the rehearsal everyone gathered in the rectory for sandwiches, cookies and soft drinks.

Annie could barely sleep that night and was up at the crack of dawn. She danced around her bedroom holding the precious dress and veil to her face, imagining herself a princess. "This will be a wonderful day for Timothy and me," she sang.

Rose had planned a special breakfast for her family and as she was putting fresh flowers on the table John came downstairs piggybacking Timothy. "He's still a little tired, perhaps because of all the excitement yesterday," he said as he placed Timothy in his chair. Annie came bouncing into the dining room, hugged Timothy and proclaimed that today was going to be a magical day for them.

They arrived at the cathedral on time and Annie took her place in the procession. She looked around for Timothy but he was not opposite her where he should have been. She stepped out of line and walked slowly to the back of the church where she found her father talking to Father O'Reilly. Timothy was standing close by. She went to her brother and took his hand.

"Why isn't Timothy in line across from me?" she asked, bewildered.

Father O'Reilly approached and explained that he had decided that Timothy would be taken to the altar first and would be there waiting for her.

"Why?" Annie demanded to know.

"Because his braces make him limp. It is best this way. The procession line has to be straight and this way it will be."

"I don't think God cares if Timothy limps and the line isn't straight. He has to be across from me. That's how it's supposed to be. That's what we planned."

"Well, that's not how it's going to be, Annie. Don't argue with me. Get back and take your place in line. The ceremony is scheduled to start in two minutes."

"No, I won't do it. Not without Timothy across from me."

She ran from the church to her mother who was waiting outside, with the priest and her father in pursuit.

"She won't listen to reason, Rose. Talk to her. She refuses to do as she is told and now the ceremony won't start on time because of her," John said, exasperated.

"Why are they doing this, Mom? Why can't Timothy go down the aisle across from me? It isn't fair."

"Sometimes life isn't fair, Annie. Now apologize to Father O'Reilly and go back and take your place."

With lowered head, Annie did as her mother asked but the magic of the day was gone.

CHAPTER 6

Life settled into a routine with Rose spending most of her day with Timothy. Sister Theresa came on Tuesdays and Thursdays after her school day to teach Timothy. During this time Rose always left them alone but kept a close eye on her. After several weeks of this, Timothy confided to his mother that he didn't like Sister Theresa and he didn't want her to come to the house anymore. When Rose questioned him, he simply said, "There is something about her. I don't trust her and I don't know why."

"You can teach me, Mom. You're so smart and I know I will learn faster."

This came as a big surprise to Rose but that evening after dinner she interrupted her husband, who was reading the newspaper, and told him Sister Theresa was no longer needed, explaining Timothy's feelings. He reluctantly agreed but was concerned that she would be taking too much time away from the other children.

"Don't be concerned with the time I spend with the children," she shot back. "You should be concerned with the lack of time you spend with them. You are never home."

He folded the newspaper and said he would talk to Sister Theresa and let her know her services were no longer needed.

The following day John made his way to the school to talk to Sister Theresa. He had mixed feelings about it, feeling that Rose was right in this case, but also liking the fact that Sister Theresa was in his home two days a week teaching his son.

He arrived shortly before the end of the school day and found Sister Theresa in her office. She stood when she saw him and held out her hands to him. He took both of them in his and told her how nice it was to see her. She immediately put on the kettle and made tea. As they settled to enjoy the tea he told her she didn't have to teach Timothy anymore, that Rose would be taking over.

"Well, I hope she is doing the right thing, John. As hard as I tried to make friends with her, she is not interested. I did notice that she keeps a beautiful home for you and the children and it was nice being there. If I can't teach Timothy then perhaps I should concentrate on Annie. She does so well with all her subjects, especially reading and penmanship, but her math will keep her from making the honor roll, I'm sorry to say."

"I wasn't aware that she wasn't doing well in math and I wonder if Rose knows; math was her best subject in school and she knows how important math is. I'll talk to her about it. She is so busy taking care of Timothy that she is stretched for time and it's just going to get tougher with a new baby on the way. If you can spare the time, we would appreciate you helping Annie."

"You're wife is pregnant?"

He smiled. "Yes, the baby is due around Christmas."

The bell was ringing, signaling the end of the school day. John looked at his watch and said, "Is my watch wrong or is school getting out early today?"

"No, there is nothing wrong with your watch. School is getting out early because of a teachers' meeting. We will be working on final exams for this school year," she said, her voice a little shaky.

"I must leave now. I still have several hours of work waiting for me at the office."

"You work so hard, John. I hope your wife appreciates you."

******

Annie was happy to be getting out of school early. As she headed for the street she saw her father's car parked nearby. She looked around and spotted him. She hollered and ran toward him.

"What are you doing here, Dad? Is everything okay, is Timothy alright?"

"Yes, Annie, everything is fine. C'mon, I'll give you a ride home."

This was the first time Annie could ever remember being alone with her father. It was an odd feeling. Her father seemed preoccupied with his thoughts on the drive home and when the silence became unbearable for her she blurted out, "Where do you go every night after dinner, Dad?"

Her father was taken aback.

"Well, young lady, that is really none of your business but I will tell you. I own several race horses and each night I go to the stables to feed and water them. They also have to be exercised and that takes a lot of time. Now does that settle your curiosity?"

"Horses! Horses!" Annie couldn't have been more surprised. "I would never have guessed that. How many do you have? Are they boys or girls? Do they have names and do you really race them? I want to go see them and I want to ride them. I could even go with you after dinner and help feed them. When can I see them?"

John chuckled. Of his three children, he was fondest of Annie. He loved her enthusiasm and the love she had for her brother. Her best feature was her platinum blonde hair, which her mother always worked into long curls and tied with a ribbon that matched the outfit she was wearing. All her spare time was spent dancing. Rose had her in ballet and tap classes and whenever anyone asked her what she was going to be when she grew up, the answer was always "a dancer." He believed this was just a phase she was going through and felt teaching would be a good profession for her. She was very artistic, just like her mother; in fact, she was very much like her mother.

"Slow down, Annie, slow down. Let's make a deal. Today Sister Theresa told me that your best subject is reading but your math is not very good. When you get an A in math I will take you to see the horses. Perhaps Sister Theresa will give you extra help after school if you ask her nicely."

"It's a deal, Dad, it's a deal. I don't like her but if getting extra help from her helps me get an A and I can go see the horses, then I'll do it."

CHAPTER 7

It was arranged the following Monday that Annie would start getting extra help with her math. She waited after school for Sister Theresa, and as she lined up her math book and ruler on her desk she realized she forgot her pencils. She ran into the cloakroom to get the pencils when she heard Sister Theresa and Sister Margaret enter the classroom.

"The last thing in the world that family needs is another baby. My God, what was John thinking? Why wasn't he more careful? What if this new baby turns out to be another Timothy? What a tragedy that would be. God only knows what goes in that house with that woman. Does she think having another baby will keep John at home? The only relief he gets is his work, his horses and coming to the convent to talk over a cup of tea."

She glanced at the classroom clock.

"Where is that child? I told her to wait for me. Obviously she doesn't want the extra help, but she certainly needs it. I only volunteered because of John. Well, I'll just call him and let him know she didn't wait. That child has no discipline and deserves a strapping for not being here."

"I don't suggest you do that," said Sister Margaret. "Remember when you did take the ruler to her and her mother's reaction. We don't want a repeat of that. We've wasted enough time here. It's time to leave."

The two nuns left the classroom together.

Annie heard the door close. She couldn't move, she was so shocked by what she had just heard. "Could it be true what Sister Theresa said?" she whispered to herself. Was her mother really having a baby and would the baby be like Timothy? And why did she call her father by his first name? Everyone called him Mr. O'Brien.

She sat there for ten minutes and finally stood up on shaky legs and made her way home.

"You're home early, Annie," her mother said as she closed the door behind her. "I thought you were going to stay after school and Sister Theresa was going to help you with math?"

"Sister Theresa wasn't there. I waited but she never came." The lie was spoken before Annie realized what she was saying. It was the first lie she had ever told and wondered if it would be the last.

"I'm going to my room, Mom, I don't feel good."

Five minutes later Rose knocked on her daughter's bedroom door and walked in. She found Annie face down, crying into her pillow. She reached for her and held her close.

"Do you want to tell me what happened today, Annie?"

"I lied to you. I'm so sorry, Mom. Sister Theresa did show up with Sister Margaret. I was in the cloakroom looking for my pencils when they came in. They said you were going to have a baby and it might be like Timothy. Why do they think something is so wrong with Timothy? Sister Theresa talked about Dad and his horses and called him by his first name. Did you know that Dad has horses? He said I could go see them if I got an A in math. I guess that will never happen I don't want her help. I don't like her."

Rose brushed back Annie's hair. "Oh, sure you will get an A in math. We can work on your math together. Now come along and help set the table for dinner."

During dinner John and Rose told their children there would be another brother or sister around Christmas time. They were very excited and talked about whether it would be a girl or boy and what they would call the new baby. Rose also made the announcement that there would be no time for the family rosary as she was going to help Annie with her math along with Timothy. John left for the stables. Kate went to her room to do her homework. She didn't need help with her lessons; the work seemed to come very easily to her. She had always been a straight-A student.

And so it began. Math lessons every night after dinner. Annie and Timothy agreed math wasn't so hard the way their mother taught it. She started by placing on the table a penny, a nickel, a dime, a quarter, a half dollar and a dollar bill. The coins represented five, ten, twenty-five and fifty, while the dollar bill was one hundred. It all made sense to Annie, using money to learn math and at the same time learning the importance and value of money.

CHAPTER 8

"Two more weeks, just two more weeks and school will be out for the summer, but today is the math test," Annie thought to herself as she sat in the classroom. "I'm sure I'll get an A."

Sister Theresa handed each of the pupils the math test and told them not to begin until she said so.

Annie sat quietly with her hands folded in her lap and waited patiently.

The nun clapped her hands together and everyone picked up their pencils and began the test. Annie looked over the test and saw there were only twenty questions. An hour later she was finished and handed in her test. Sister Theresa said nothing, just nodded her head and excused Annie for the day.

As Annie quietly closed the classroom door the nun picked up a red marking pencil. Before starting to mark the test she glanced down at the answers and couldn't believe her eyes. She had no need for the marking pencil because Annie had answered all the questions correctly. Her hands started to shake; she could not believe her eyes. "She had to have cheated," the nun thought. When the last pupil handed in her test, she immediately went to the office and telephoned Annie's father and asked him to meet with her the next day after school. "It's about Annie's test," she offered in explanation.

The following day everyone was seated in the classroom, waiting anxiously and excitedly for the test results. After the papers were handed back to the pupils, there was much whispering among the girls as to who passed and who didn't; everyone except Annie.

She raised her hand but was ignored by Sister Theresa. She left her desk and walked up to the nun and asked for her test score.

"You will get yours at the end of the day. Your father will be here after school. Now go sit down."

The recess bell rang and the girls filed out to the schoolyard to play their games, but Annie kept on walking.

She pounded her feet on the pavement and with every step chanted, "I hate that nun, I really hate her." By the time she reached home, she had calmed down and told her mother why she was home. "Sister Theresa wouldn't give me my test. I know I did really well, why wouldn't she give it to me? I asked her and all she said was she called Dad and he is coming to see her after school."

"Annie, you can't just leave school without a good reason. I'll write a note to Sister Margaret apologizing for you leaving. I'm sure she is wondering where you are. I can't drive you back because I can't leave Timothy alone. Now hurry back and I'll see you after school."

Annie took the note and ran back to school.

Once she was gone, Rose called her husband to ask why he was meeting with Sister Theresa.

"I don't think it's anything important, just something about Annie's math test. I'll see you at dinner."

All morning Rose wondered what was going on at Annie's school. She knew Kate would be home from school early and she could watch Timothy because Rose had every intention of being at that meeting.

******

"John, it is impossible to believe that she got every question right on that test. Just impossible," Sister Theresa said as she paced back and forth, the dusty chalk residue on the floor powdering the hem of her black habit. "She hasn't had any extra help for months and months and she aces the test. I insist she write another test."

Annie sat silently in her chair as Sister Theresa ranted to her father. Finally she could take no more. She stood up and faced the nun.

"Why did you call Dad to school? Why didn't you call my mother? She would tell you how I aced the test. Dad doesn't know, he's never at home. He's too busy with his horses."

Calmly she walked toward the door and turned.

"I didn't cheat on the test and I'm not taking another one. I'm going home."

Sister Theresa moved quickly, almost catching her long beads on the desk. She grabbed Annie from behind and flung her into a nearby chair. Annie saw the hand coming down and felt the blow to her face. The nun's hand was raised to strike again but was caught in mid-air.

The rage showed on Rose's face as her nails dug into the nun's wrist. She twisted her around and shoved her into the desk. The startled nun screamed, "You weren't invited to this meeting, now get out of here. John, tell her to leave."

"I told you before never to touch my daughter."

John stood up, holding his head as the two women faced each other.

"Rose, what are you doing here?" he asked.

"Is that all you have to say. This woman just attacked your daughter and you can only wonder why I'm here? I'm protecting my daughter, which is what you should be doing."

She took Annie's hand and brushed the tears off her confused face and led her out of the school.

"Oh, my God, Theresa, what have you done?" John said.

"I shouldn't have hit her but she was being disrespectful. I know she cheated on that test. I know I'm right."

"No, you're not, Theresa. Rose has been working with Annie for months on her math. She didn't cheat. Annie would never cheat. With Rose's help she caught onto math quickly and loves it. Annie isn't the one you should be concerned about right now. It's Rose you've got to worry about and you don't want to be a victim of her wrath."

"Your wife doesn't worry me. She can't do anything."

CHAPTER 9

The phone in the rectory was ringing insistently. Father O'Reilly called for his housekeeper, Helga, but there was no answer. He put down his Scotch and pushed himself out of the chair while reaching for the phone. He had known this call would be coming and knew it wouldn't be pleasant.

"St. Peter's Church. Father O'Reilly speaking."

"Michael, this is Rose O'Brien. I will be at the rectory this evening at seven o'clock."

"I'd like to see you, Rose, but I'll be in a meeting at that time. However, I can see you in a day or so. I'll have my secretary call you tomorrow to set up an appointment."

"No, you will see me at seven o'clock tonight and if you are not there I will find you." She hung up.

Father O'Reilly put the receiver into the cradle of the telephone and turned to his two companions. He raised his drink and said, "She sounded very calm and that is more frightening than anything."

He picked up the bottle of Scotch and topped up John's and Sister Theresa's drink.

"Don't worry," he said smiling. "I've handled tougher women than her."

At seven o'clock sharp, Rose rang the bell at the rectory. Helga answered and directed her into the sitting area. Rose sat near a stand of lighted votive candles, their flames dancing over the crosses hanging on the wall. There were three empty glasses and an ashtray with cigar butts on a side table. The room had that church odor, mixed with the smell of cigars, and it made her stomach turn. "What a depressing place," she thought.

Father O'Reilly entered the room quietly and his eyes focused on Rose. She was a very pretty woman and hadn't changed much over the years. They weren't friends in high school, she being a couple of years behind him. He remembered she had a great talent for art and received several awards for her paintings, and he recalled she wasn't very social but friendly. But now she wasn't very friendly or social; she was on a mission.

"What can I do for you, Rose? Can I pour you a drink?"

"No, thank you. I won't take up much of your time. What I have to say won't take long."

"Surely you're not here regarding that little misunderstanding over Annie's test score. You must admit, Rose, Annie has always had trouble with math. You can't blame Sister Theresa for suspecting she cheated."

"I'm not here to discuss that. There would be no point. You've already had that discussion with John and Sister Theresa.

He looked at her, raising one eyebrow.

"Don't give me that look, Michael. They've already been here. Your housekeeper neglected to pick up the glasses and ashtray." She glanced toward the side table.

"I'm here to tell you that Sister Theresa is to be removed from the school and if I really push it, out of the diocese."

"You're being ridiculous. Nothing of the sort is going to happen."

"Yes, it will. St. Peter's parish does not need a lawsuit and I will bring one against the church for assaulting my daughter. Just ask my husband if this can be done. Which side do you think he will take? The school's or his daughter's? The school year ends in two weeks. She is not to be back here next term."

"Rose, be reasonable. You're making a big mistake. We can work this out."

"Michael, I don't expect you to understand. You've never had children... or have you?" She paused and stared right through him.

As Rose picked up her purse and left the rectory, Father O'Reilly walked to the side table and poured himself a stiff drink.

CHAPTER 10

The school year ended and Annie's math test with the bright red A+ and gold star was taped to the refrigerator for all to see. There was a party in the garden with fresh lemonade, sandwiches and cake. Timothy was having a good day and joined in watching from his wheelchair, with Annie close by.

The summer passed quickly and the new school year started. Annie reported that Sister Theresa was no longer at St. Peter's and no one knew where she had gone.

"Mom, did you know Sister Theresa isn't at the school anymore? I wonder where she went."

In the following months Annie excelled in school, knowing she wouldn't have to worry about Sister Theresa again. One evening she was sitting at the kitchen table doing homework with Timothy when Rose leaned over to help them and felt a stab of pain. "It's time," Rose thought. "It's time."

It was a long night for the family but early the next morning they welcomed a howling, healthy baby boy into the world. He was given the name Joseph Daniel. From the moment he came home, Annie was captivated by him. She would stare at her little brother while he was sleeping and pray he would walk. Months later she held his little hands and walked him around the house and before long he was walking and running on his own.

As Rose watched the progression of her baby boy, she was also watching the decline of Timothy. He could do very little for himself now but he never complained. It tore her heart to pieces as she wondered how much longer she would have him. She did what she could to make him comfortable but the hours she spent working on his wasting muscles, working on his hands to keep them open, seemed fruitless. He was getting weaker and weaker and there wasn't a damn thing she could do to stop the dreaded disease from destroying his muscles. She again recalled the exact words of the medical team: "It's an atrophy, a wasting of the muscles." It was called muscular dystrophy, but Rose called it hell.

There was another form of hell being raised in the O'Brien household. Kate, who was graduating from high school, wanted to become a doctor. She graduated with honors and had received a scholarship. Annie was ecstatic and positive that when Kate became a doctor she would find a cure for Timothy and he would walk again.

But her father wasn't as enthusiastic. "Women don't become doctors. That's no career for a woman. It's a waste of time and money because they eventually get married and have children and they don't work anymore. It's okay for them to become nurses and that's what Kate will do. It takes half the time and half the money. She can go to school right here in the city. She will still be able to help out at home. She has a car so she can travel back and forth to school and remain living at home. I will pay for nursing but not medical school, and now there will be no more discussion on the subject."

Annie was upset by this decision and pleaded with her mother. "Mom, it isn't fair that Kate can't become a doctor. There has to be a way. Is it because Dad doesn't want to spend the money? If he doesn't have enough money then he should sell his horses. Kate is more important than the horses. And speaking of the horses, Dad broke his promise to me. I still haven't seen them."

Rose laughed out loud and hugged her daughter. Still laughing, she said, "Don't you worry about it, Annie, there's more than one way to skin a cat."

Kate filled out the application for nursing school but her mother had a different application for her. "There's no sense in applying to medical school, Mom," Kate cried. "Dad said no and I need more than a scholarship to get through medical school."

"There are other ways, Kate. Don't give up on your dreams. Don't let anyone stand in your way, not even your father."

CHAPTER 11

The house was quiet after John had left to tend to his horses and the children were upstairs in their bedrooms settling down for the night.

Rose checked the time and realized it was later than she thought but she picked up the telephone and made the call that she had been planning throughout the day.

"St. Peter's Rectory," the voice on the other end said.

"This is Mrs. O'Brien and I would like to speak to Father O'Reilly, please."

"One moment, please," Rose heard Helga calling for the priest and soon he picked up the receiver.

"Hello, Rose. This is rather late for you to be calling so it must be important. It seems the only time you call is when you want something, so what is it this time?"

"I want to meet with you tomorrow morning."

"Morning Mass will be over at ten thirty and I can see you after that."

"I'll be there at eleven."

At eleven o'clock sharp the next morning Rose rang the rectory bell. The priest answered the door and invited her in. Coffee and biscuits were laid out on the side table and the priest poured coffee and handed her a cup.

"What's on your mind, Rose?" he asked.

"I'm here to ask the diocese to grant Kate a full scholarship."

"She already has a scholarship. She doesn't need a full scholarship. John can certainly pay for her nursing school at St. Mary's," he said as he topped up his coffee and sank his teeth into a biscuit.

"I'm aware of that and I'm also aware of other things," Rose said, staring at him. "Kate wants to study medicine and she will."

"What do you mean by other things, Rose?"

"How is Sister Theresa, Michael?"

The priest's coffee cup rattled in the saucer.

"Why do you care how she is? You got what you wanted; she's no longer at St. Peter's. How she is doing is no concern of yours."

"I know what's going on, Michael. Let me know when the scholarship is in place."

"I'll see what I can do and get back to you this afternoon."

The afternoon seemed to drag on but Rose was very confident Kate would get the scholarship.

At four o'clock the phone rang.

"I'll get it," shouted Annie. "It's for you, Mom. It's Father O'Reilly."

Rose took the phone and was told Kate would have a full scholarship. She hung up and smiled, but she also knew her husband would still be against it.

"Are you okay, Mom? You have a funny look on your face."

"Yes, I'm fine, dear. Just thinking about how much I'll miss Kate."

"Kate isn't going that far away, Mom. She'll be home and besides I'll get my learner's permit soon and be able to drive. I'll run your errands and do your shopping just like Kate. Don't worry."

John was home early and was not in a good mood. He was very quiet during dinner but as soon as the children were in their rooms, he laid his cards on the table. "Michael called me this afternoon. I told you from the beginning that Kate wouldn't be going to medical school but somehow you convinced Michael to get a full scholarship for her."

"We can talk about this, John. Let me pour you a drink." She handed him a Scotch on the rocks and sat next to him.

"What really bothers you about Kate studying medicine? You have to realize that times are changing. We are heading into the 1960s and things are opening up for women. You have to accept that, John. It's going to be hard to send her off to university in Montreal but we have to think of what she wants."

"What do you mean she will be going to university in Montreal? Michael told me she would be going to St. Mary's; he is not aware she is going to Montreal. You're wrong. She's going to St. Mary's."

"St. Mary's was never mentioned when I was talking to him," Rose said. "That was a big assumption on his part."

"Well, that certainly changes things regarding money. Where do you think the money is going to come from for her living expenses? I'm not made of money."

"The church sent a tax statement of your contributions for the past year. It was addressed to both of us so I opened it. You gave ten thousand dollars to the church last year. You can cut that in half. And you seem to have enough money to keep your horses, which is a big expense. So, what's more important to you, the church, your horses or your daughter's education?"

"You can't tell me what to do with my money. Who do you think you are? You're my wife, you take orders from me."

"Talk it over with your buddy Michael and Sister Theresa. They seem to be the ones you discuss everything with instead of your wife."

Timothy was calling for his mother and Rose went to him.

John fell back into the chair. He wondered what she knew and how much. Maybe he should start spending more time at home. Rose was a good woman and an excellent mother. She created a beautiful home and life was blissful until Timothy was diagnosed with the dreaded disease.

He remembered how infatuated he was with Rose when they met at St. Mary's University. He was twenty-one years old and she was nineteen. He was in his third year of Law and she in the first year of Arts. She had dreams to be a great artist and she certainly had the talent, but that was all put aside when she told him she was pregnant. He will never forget that day. They went to his school friend Michael, who had just been ordained a priest, and he married them quietly. Together they told their shocked parents and no one asked if she was pregnant; they just counted the months. Kate was born five months later, weighing a mere four and a half pounds. It was a premature birth, everyone said; they didn't have to get married. They dropped to their knees in a prayer of thanks. Rose didn't return to school but devoted herself to the baby. When she felt Kate was in good health she got a job at the local art gallery to help make ends meet, and her mother took care of the baby. Those early years were good.

When John graduated with his law degree he was taken on at the largest firm in town. Being the junior lawyer, he worked very long hours but Rose was always waiting for him when he got home. She would warm up a plate of homemade spaghetti and open a bottle of Chianti and they would talk about their day while Kate slept. Those were the lean years and although they didn't have very much, they had each other. He was so in love with her. She was petite and smart and she loved to dance. Maybe that's where Annie got her love for the dance. When Kate was three years old, Rose became pregnant with Timothy. He remembered getting the call at work that Rose was in labor and he rushed to St. Joseph's Hospital where he held his son for the first time. Things gradually changed after that.

Rose was no longer waiting for him to get home from work. Her day was filled with taking care of a three-year-old and a newborn. He spent more time at the office and there were nights when he would stop in at the rectory and visit with his old friend, Father O'Reilly. Some evenings Theresa would also be there.

They were a threesome in high school and everyone thought he and Theresa would eventually end up together, but he met Rose and loved for the first time. Shortly after he met Rose, Theresa entered the convent.

He was now thirty-nine years old and felt he had been a good father and husband. His family never lacked for anything. Rose had everything she wanted and got what she wanted. She certainly got Kate into medical school.

He made good money but with the horses and all the extra expenses he had been incurring recently, things were getting tight and would be even tighter with Kate at university. He knew he would figure it out.

CHAPTER 12

Excitement was in the air as Kate was packing all she would need for university. Timothy sat in his chair as clothes were ironed and packed and decisions made on what to take. Annie was dancing around the room to her favorite music and little Joey was standing and stomping his tiny feet as he clung to the wheel of Timothy's chair. "He's going to be walking pretty soon, Mom," Annie said.

Rose looked over at her four children and counted her blessings, thinking there was only one thing missing: their father. This was Kate's last night at home and he should have been there. Did he even remember? He didn't remember to pick up Timothy's prescription on his way home from the office.

She turned to Kate and said, "I have to run to the drug store to pick up Timothy's prescription. I won't be long."

"I'll go for you, Mom. I need a break from all this ironing and folding of clothes. Do you want to come for the ride, Annie?"

Kate backed the car out of the garage and headed for the store.

"I'm really going to miss you, Kate," Annie said sadly. "I really hope I can help Mom as much as you do and I'm really worried about starting high school. All the nuns will expect me to be as smart as you but I'm not."

"You are smart, Annie, and don't worry about the nuns. Just be yourself. I heard there is a new principal and she is starting a dance program that you can take. You'll have your driver's license soon and be able to help Mom. You worry too much. Everything is going to be fine."

They picked up the prescription and headed home when Annie asked, "Do you think Dad is at the stables? He told me a long time ago that he would show me the horses but he never did. He's just too busy."

"He might be there. The stables aren't very far from here. Let's go see if he's there. But we will have to call Mom and let her know." Kate turned onto the road that led to the Acres Stables, which were only about twenty minutes away. She had only been there once and promised herself she would never go again but here she was taking Annie.

They entered the gates and drove up a long driveway lined with oak trees. The sun was just setting and it seemed so peaceful. She remembered where her father's horses were stabled and as they rounded the corner Kate saw her father's car parked in his assigned space. "There's Dad's car," she said and parked next to it.

"You wait here, Annie, while I go find him."

Kate entered the stable, walking toward her father's area, where she knew he would be, and knocked on the door.

There was the sound of chairs being pushed back, feet hurrying across the floor and the crash of glass. She heard her father say to whomever he was with that he wasn't expecting anyone and wondered who could possibly be at the door.

"It's me, Dad. It's Kate, and Annie is with me."

"I'll be right there, just give me a minute."

Her father unlocked the door and stepped out, pushing his dark, thick hair back into place. He smiled, closing the door behind him.

"What a surprise. Does your mother know you're here?"

"Yes, Mom knows and Annie wants to see the horses. We don't have a lot of time as I have to get back with Timothy's prescription."

He put his hand to his forehead, remembering that he forgot to pick up his son's medication.

Annie was out of the car and stood beside Kate. She took her sister's hand. Her father reached for her other hand and said, "Come along, Annie, and I'll show you the horses." They walked through the stable, her father telling Annie the name of each horse. They came to a newborn colt named Little Annie. "I named her Little Annie after you and she is going to be a winner just like you, Annie," he said.

As they were leaving, Annie spotted another door marked Tack Room.

"What's in there?"

"Oh, that's where all the harnesses and equipment are kept for the horses. He slowly opened the tack room door and she poked her inquisitive head inside.

"This is nice but there's a lot of stuff in here. You even have a leather couch and chair and other furniture. You could almost live here, but what is that smell?"

"That's just the smell of the horses. Now you and Kate had better get back home. Your mother will be getting worried. Tell her I'll be home soon."

As Kate drove away, she looked into the rear view mirror and saw only darkness except for her father standing under the stable lamp as he stared after the car.

"Well, Annie, what did you think of the horses?" Kate asked.

"They are really beautiful but I had a funny feeling being there and the smell bothered me."

"The smell is just the horses."

"No, Kate, it was something else. It smelt like perfume."

Dr. White's car and an ambulance were parked in the driveway when they arrived home. Rose met them at the door and explained that Timothy had a bad spell and couldn't breathe. He would be spending the night in the hospital and she would be staying with him.

"Dr. White said this is just a precaution, just being on the safe side and he will be home tomorrow," Rose said in a very calm voice, but Kate noticed her hands were shaking.

They watched as the ambulance pulled away. "They should put the siren and lights on," Annie said. "Timothy would like that."

A week later Timothy came home with an emergency breathing apparatus, which frightened Annie.

CHAPTER 13

The week after Kate left, Rose took Annie to the police station to get her learner's permit to drive. She was waving the permit around Timothy when her father came home. He wanted to know what all the fuss was about.

"Annie just got her learner's permit," Timothy said. Annie handed it to her father.

"Well, c'mon, let me give you your first lesson."

"Don't be long," Rose said. "Dinner will be ready shortly."

A half hour later they were back and Annie was shaking.

"How did it go?" Timothy asked.

"It's not as easy as it looks. There are so many things to remember. I think I'm going to need a lot of lessons and practice. I asked Dad what car I should watch out for and he said to watch the car that's behind the one in front of me. It took me a minute to figure that one out. I always noticed when Dad drives he has one foot on the brake and one on the gas. I did the same thing and he went a little crazy and told me not to do as he does but as he says. I'll remember that."

On the first day of high school Annie drove with her father by her side. She was improving, he told her. On the front door of the school was a notice that all students should assemble in the auditorium. Annie followed the signs and saw many familiar faces from her old school. A bell rang and everyone became quiet as the principal,

Sister Catherine, welcomed everyone. The students were assigned their home classroom and as Annie made her way to Room 121, Sister Catherine stopped her in the hall and introduced herself.

"Welcome, Annie. I hope you will be happy here."

Annie shook her hand and looked into eyes that were smiling back at her. Despite the coif surrounding the nun's face, Annie saw her beauty and felt she looked vaguely familiar. A feeling of happiness and belonging came over her.

Sister Catherine took her under her wing and over the months Annie's grades flourished but her heart was always in the dance class. All her spare time was devoted to practicing for the Christmas pageant. She was transforming from a skinny little girl into a young lady with poise and charm. Annie wondered if she could be any happier. Her sixteenth birthday was around the corner and she would be getting her driver's license. Driving to and from school would give her more time to spend with Sister Catherine, whom she adored and trusted. She was sure her Christmas report card would have straight A's.

On the morning of the pageant, Annie practiced her routine over and over for Timothy. He was her biggest fan. Front row seats had been arranged for the family and Timothy would be there, watching her every step. Kate was home for Christmas and had driven Annie to the school in the early afternoon for one last rehearsal.

"C'mon, everyone, we don't want to be late," Rose said as she helped Joey into his coat.

John was carrying Timothy to the car when he went limp in his father's arms.

Turning, he rushed back to the house, calling for Rose. "Oh, my God, Rose, what's wrong with Timothy?"

"Lay him on the chesterfield," Rose said calmly.

She loosened Timothy's tie, felt for his pulse and started pounding him on the back — pounding life into him. She looked up into her husband's face and saw a look of hopelessness. Timothy's eyes opened and he coughed.

"What happened, Mom? I had a bad pain in my chest and I guess I passed out. Can we still go see Annie?" he mumbled.

"I don't think so, son. I'm going to call Dr. White and have him come take a look at you. John, you take Kate and Joey to the performance. Annie will understand."

Dr. White arrived within minutes of Rose's call and examined Timothy, who seemed exhausted and fell asleep in his mother's arms. She gently placed his head on the pillow and left the room with the doctor.

"It's not good, Rose. The disease is progressing at a steady rate. The pain Timothy felt was his heart. Statistically, he has lived longer than most afflicted with this terrible disease. Despite the care and enormous love you have given him, the day is nearing when the illness will win. You have to prepare yourself," he said gently.

"Can a mother ever prepare herself for her child's untimely death? Even when you know it is inevitable? It is so unfair," she said as she led the doctor to the front door.

After the performance, there was a reception for the students and guests. Annie spotted her family as they entered the room. "Where are Mom and Timothy? I didn't see them when I was on stage."

Her father handed Joey off to Kate and walked toward Sister Catherine, who was talking to a woman.

Kate explained to Annie that Timothy had a bad spell and their mother decided to stay at home. Annie immediately called after her father and started walking toward him. He met her halfway. "I want to go home right now and see Timothy." They turned to leave and John looked over his shoulder.

"Who is that woman with Sister Catherine? Do you know her?" asked Annie.

"I was just congratulating Sister Catherine on the success of the pageant. Now, let's go."

When they got home, Annie burst into the house close to tears. "How is Timothy, Mom, is he okay?"

"Yes, Annie, he is going to be okay. He's sleeping. He was very disappointed he didn't see you dancing tonight but tomorrow is Christmas Eve and while we're putting up the tree you can dance for him."

"Now tell me everything about tonight. Kate says you dazzled the crowd."

"I did okay but there is something bothering me. When we were leaving, Dad was talking to a woman who looked familiar to me and I asked him who she was but he didn't give me an answer."

"It's getting late, Annie, and you must be tired. Let's turn in for the night," Rose said as she put her arm around her daughter, avoiding the question, and walked her to her room.

As Rose was putting out the lights, John came to her and said he was going to the office to finish some work.

CHAPTER 14

"Sweet Sixteen" banners were hung in the ballroom of the Shadow Villa where Annie's birthday would be celebrated. Of the hundred and twenty guests invited Annie knew only a handful. Most were business associates of her father's, relatives Annie hadn't seen for years and everyone from the church.

She made her entrance on her father's arm, dressed in an ivory chiffon tea-length gown with a turquoise sash. Her platinum hair was pulled back and held in place with a diamond clip that was her birthday gift from her father.

Father O'Reilly blessed the party and as he raised his hand in blessing he took a second look at Annie and realized she was no longer a little girl but a beautiful young woman.

Timothy was sitting by himself and Annie walked toward him. She was stunned at how thin he had become. He seemed to be leaning to the side of his wheelchair and as she reached him she straightened him up. "Who was that good-looking fellow you were dancing with a short while ago? The tall, handsome one in the dark suit?" he asked.

"Oh, that's Mark Cohen and he's the son of one of Dad's partners. I really like him; he's a great dancer." She called Mark over and introduced him to Timothy.

Although the party was a great success, and as grateful as Annie was, she was more excited to get her driver's license the following day. She met her father at the police station and passed the test easily. No one was surprised she passed as there was no one more determined than Annie. After dinner that night Rose and John told her they had a surprise birthday gift for her. They covered her eyes with a silk scarf and lead her outside. When the scarf was removed, standing before her was a bright red convertible with Timothy sitting in the front seat. She screamed with joy, jumped in the car and hugged her brother.

"We are going to have the summer of our lives, Timothy. You just wait and see. I can't believe this, I am so happy!"

Timothy had trouble sitting in the car so a series of belts and straps was installed along with a headrest to keep him upright. Each day they would go for a drive but, despite everything that had been done for Timothy's comfort, as the summer days passed each became shorter as he tired very quickly. On one of their last summer days Annie decided to take him to see their father's horses. It had been awhile since she had been to the stables but she felt pretty confident she would find the way. She also knew her father wouldn't be there in the afternoon but his horse trainer would be and he could show Timothy around.

She found the stable and was surprised to see her father's car there.

She knocked on the door but there was no answer. She lifted the latch, pulled the door open and stepped inside. "Dad, are you here?" she called. No answer. The tack room door was ajar so she pushed it open slightly and as she did she saw the shadow of a man and woman embracing. She wondered who they were and what they were doing in her dad's tack room. She closed the door and turned to leave when she heard her father's voice.

"Annie, is that you?" he asked as the tack room door swung open. "What are you doing here?"

"I brought Timothy to see the horses. What are you doing here? Shouldn't you be at work? Who is that woman in there that you were hugging?"

"Don't be silly, Annie, there is no woman here. You probably just saw shadows of the saddles and bridles. You have such an imagination. Now, let's bring Timothy in and show him around."

Timothy loved everything about the horses — the smell of the oats, the leather saddles, the rub-down liniment and of course the horses themselves — but too soon it was time to go. John lifted him into the car, secured him with the belts, and folded and placed the wheelchair in the trunk of Annie's car.

"Are you going to leave the top down, Annie?" her father asked. "It looks like it might rain." Annie didn't reply, but perhaps she should have listened because halfway home the clouds burst open and sheets of rain fell. She scrambled to get the top up and wiped the rain off Timothy's face.

"I hate the rain. Someday I will live where the sky is always blue and sunny and I will take Timothy with me," she thought. She was also thinking of Sister Catherine and needed to go see her. She took Timothy home and left for the convent.

Sister Catherine met her at the convent door. "I was surprised but delighted to receive your call but what could be so urgent that you had to see me this evening?" She led Annie into the reception area. It seemed very ghostly to Annie. The high twenty-foot ceilings, the echo of your footsteps as you walked across the wooden floor and everyone whispering. It was too quiet. Votive candles in ruby red containers burned with barely a flicker of the flame.

"Sit down, Annie, and tell me what has got you so worried."

"Sister, I think my father is cheating on my mother. I took Timothy to see his horses today and he was there when he should have been at work. I saw the shadow of a woman hugging him although Dad said it was my imagination. He said it was the shadows of the stuff in the tack room that I saw but I know differently. I don't know what to do. Should I tell Mom?"

"Oh, Annie, your father would never cheat on your mother. He's a good Catholic man who lives by the doctrines and commandments of the church. What you saw had to have been shadows. Did you ask him why he was at the stables?"

"Yes, he said he came out to check on one of the horses that was sick but they all looked pretty healthy to me."

"Well, that's it. Now you get all those thoughts out of your mind and start thinking about the year ahead. Grade eleven is not easy but I will be there to give you all the extra help you need. You will also have to start thinking about university and what you want to study. Hopefully you will choose St. Mary's, unlike your sister. Father O'Reilly was very upset with Kate for not going to St. Mary's. You can also join the CYO this year. They have wonderful programs and a dance every Friday night. Now, run along home and don't worry about your father. He is a good man."

As Annie drove home, Sister Catherine's words kept going through her mind but she still felt something was wrong and decided to call Kate when she got home. However, she had little success. As she placed the telephone receiver in the cradle the phone rang.

"Hello," said Annie.

"Hello, Annie, this is Mark Cohen. I was wondering if you would like to go out this Friday night. There is a dance at the Orchid Pavilion. It's a great place on the lake and it wouldn't be a late night. I would have you home by midnight."

"I would love to go but don't you have to be eighteen to get in?"

"Yes, but this is a special dance for sixteen- to eighteen-year-olds to celebrate the end of summer vacation," he said.

"I will ask Mom and get back to you," Annie said as she hung up the phone and went to Timothy.

"Remember that fellow I introduced you to at my party? Mark Cohen. Well, he just called and invited me to a dance this Friday night. I'm excited. I hope Mom says it's okay for me to go. Say a prayer for me," she whispered as she went in search of her mother.

"Yes, I remember Mark," Rose said when Annie told her about the invitation. "It's fine with me, Annie, but you should also talk to your father about this. He will be home shortly and you can ask him then. He still thinks you're too young to date but he may make an exception this time because he works with Mark's father." Rose smiled at her.

At dinner that night Annie blurted out that Mark had asked her to a dance. Her father put down his fork in utter surprise.

"Absolutely not. You're too young to date and even if you weren't, you couldn't go out with Mark Cohen. What were you thinking, Rose, when you said it was alright with you? Mark is a Jew; she can't go out with him. There will be no more discussion on the subject." He left the table, grabbed his keys and went out the door.

Annie picked up the phone and dialed Mark's number. "Hi Mark, this is Annie, and I would love to go to the dance with you on Friday night."

CHAPTER 15

"Are you sure you're doing the right thing, Annie?" Timothy looked concerned. "If Dad finds out he will ground you for life. You have never disobeyed him, why now?"

"Because he is wrong, Timothy. Just because Mark doesn't belong to our church doesn't mean the church he belongs to is wrong. The Catholics are no better than the Jews. Why is Dad so judgemental? Mark isn't good enough to be my friend but it's okay for Dad to work with his father. That makes no sense to me. I'll be home by midnight as I promised Mom and will tell you all about it tomorrow."

Mark introduced Annie to his friends and they danced the night away. On the drive home Mark mentioned that he was going to the horse races the next day and asked if she would like to come along. Annie said she would like to go, and take her brother, but they would have to go in her car. "My car has a special harness for Timothy and you will have to sit in the back if that's okay with you," Annie explained.

The next day, Mark arrived on time and helped settle Timothy in the car. He was very tall and strong for his eighteen years and he gently picked up Timothy from his wheelchair and placed him in his seat. Annie secured the straps as Mark put the wheelchair in the trunk of the car.

It was a hot day and Annie forgot to bring hats for Timothy and herself. "We won't be able to stay too long because of the heat, but Dad's horses are in the first two races so we can at least get to see them race," she said as they pushed Timothy up to the fence.

"And they're off," shouted the announcer.

"Which horse is Dad's?" Timothy asked.

"The jockey wearing the brown and gold colors. He's riding Brewster and is in second position. They're coming around the final turn, Timothy and I think he is going to win."

"He won, he won!" Annie shouted. "Too bad we're not old enough to bet. We would have won some money."

Annie looked toward the winner's circle and saw her father. She started to push Timothy toward the group of people standing with their father when she noticed a woman standing beside him, looking up at him and smiling.

"That's the woman," Annie thought. "Who is she? She looks so familiar but I can't place her. She's the woman who was with Dad when I went to the stables. I knew it wasn't my imagination."

Out loud, she said, "Dad's busy, Timothy, let's go home."

CHAPTER 16

When Annie entered grade eleven, she had a different attitude. She was self-assured and confident that she would get straight A's this year. During the first day Sister Catherine took her aside and laid out the days and time for tutoring in math and English. "We will build up your grades and you will have no trouble getting into St. Mary's," she said. "Your father told me that you would be studying for your teacher's degree."

"I don't know why he would tell you that, we have never talked about what I want to be. And I didn't know you knew my father."

Father O'Reilly was walking toward them.

"I'm glad you're here, Annie," he said. "I want to remind you that the CYO Council is having their annual meeting to elect new members. I have suggested to them that you would make an ideal president. The meeting is this Wednesday at six o'clock and I would like to see you there."

"I have no intention of running for any office, but I thank you for considering me. I just don't have the time. Now I have to get to class, please excuse me."

At dinner that evening her father was not in a good mood. Annie kept up idle chatter with her mother and brother waiting for the hammer to fall because she was sure Father O'Reilly had called her father.

Finally, he asked, "What's going on with you, Annie? Father O'Reilly called and told me he wanted you to run for president of the CYO but you refused. What good reason could you possibly have?"

"I told Father O'Reilly I don't have the time. Sister Catherine has set up a schedule for tutoring and any spare time I have I want to spend on my dancing. There are lot of other students who would love to be president and would do a better job. Why does Father O'Reilly call you for every little thing; doesn't he know you're busy? I don't like him and want as little to do with him as possible. Just because he's a priest and your friend doesn't mean I have to like him."

Everyone was shocked at Annie's words.

Pushing her chair back, she excused herself from the table and went to her room.

"What in the name of God has got into your daughter?" John demanded of Rose. "I don't even know her anymore. How dare she speak to me like that? She is to be grounded, all privileges taken away including her car. I've had enough."

He threw down his serviette, grabbed his keys and left. He had been doing a lot of that lately.

After he left, Timothy burst out laughing. "She sure isn't like the rest, Mom. Sometimes she frightens me the way she speaks her mind."

Little Joey excused himself from the table and said, "I want to be like Annie when I grow up."

No privileges were taken away. Rose was in charge of her children.

CHAPTER 17

Three weeks into the school year, a notice was posted for the first CYO Dance.

"The first CYO dance of the season is in a couple of weeks, Mom, and I plan on inviting Mark. He can meet my friends and I know we'll have a good time."

"Oh, Annie, that is not a very good idea. Your father will find out you have been seeing him and life will be unbearable."

"I don't really care, Mom. I think he is more concerned about what people will think than he is about me," she said as she ran her fingers through her long blonde hair.

Over the next two weeks the talk at school was all about the dance, what everyone would wear and who would be their date. Annie didn't mention Mark and already knew what she was wearing.

The afternoon of the dance Mark called to say he would not be able to pick Annie up because of a family commitment but he would meet her there at 9:00 pm and she told him she would meet him at the front entrance.

She drove herself to the dance but was sad that Timothy couldn't come; maybe next time.

She parked her car and walked toward the building where a huge banner was waving in the breeze. "Welcome to the Catholic Youth Organization Dance"

Father O'Malley was greeting everyone as they arrived. Annie didn't recognize him and thought he must be new. He extended his hand to her and said, "You must be Annie O'Brien. I know your father very well; we went to school together. He told me you would be coming but he didn't tell me what a beautiful daughter he had."

Annie smiled and shook his hand. He held her hand a little too long in her opinion. Another priest she wasn't going to like. She looked toward the ballroom and spotted her friends and excused herself from Father O'Malley.

The room was magnificently decorated in fall colors with enormous baskets of autumn leaves and flowers. There had to be at least a hundred and twenty students from three different Catholic schools. Annie spotted her closest friend, Nancy, who was standing with a group of girls from their school.

"I'm glad you're here, Annie. You can teach us how to do the twist." The music started and the girls started dancing the latest craze. Father O'Malley took Annie aside and told her they were not to do the twist as it was not an appropriate dance for young ladies. She turned to him and as she did she saw Mark enter the room.

She ran toward him smiling and reached for his hand. "I'm so glad you're here. C'mon, I want you to meet my friends." But before she could, Father O'Malley stopped her and took her aside again. "This dance is for members of the CYO only. Your friend is going to have to leave."

"Why is that, Father O'Malley? My friend Nancy brought a guest and he is not a member of the CYO."

"You know perfectly well what I mean, Annie. He has to leave."

"If he leaves, then I leave also and I won't ever be back." Mark realized what was happening and he went to Annie. She took his hand and with heads held high they walked out of the CYO together.

Outside Annie apologized to Mark. He leaned over and kissed her.

"Don't fret about it. This is not the first time this has happened. There are a lot of places where Jewish people are not welcome and this is just another one. The country club your father belongs to my father can't join, not even to golf, but everyone is welcome at the Jewish country club, which, by the way, has a much better golf course," he said laughing, trying to lighten Annie's mood. "I'll call you tomorrow and we'll go see a movie."

The more Annie thought about it on the drive home, the more furious she became. Bursting into the house, she called for her mother and blurted out everything that had happened.

She didn't know her father was in the other room.

"Can you believe it, Mom, that awful Father O'Malley telling me Mark couldn't stay at the dance? I know it had nothing to do with him not being a member; it had everything to do with him being Jewish. And do you know the country club Dad belongs to, Mark's father can't go there because he is Jewish. Why would Dad join a club that doesn't allow people of a different religion? He can't know this; he wouldn't belong to such a club. Would he, Mom?"

Rose hugged her daughter and realized that Annie just had her first taste of the real world. She looked up to see John standing in the doorway.

"I said you weren't to see Mark Cohen. If you had listened to me, none of this would have happened. You just go off and do whatever you want regardless of the consequences. I hope you have learned your lesson."

She glared at her father. "Oh, yes, I've learned. I've learned that you and your cronies at the church are a bunch of hypocrites. They preach about being good Christians, helping your fellow man, treating people equally but yet a good Jewish person is asked to leave a sacred Catholic building and then to top that off I find out my own father belongs to a club where Jews are not permitted. I will never go to the CYO or the country club again and if I didn't like Sister Catherine so much I would refuse to go to a Catholic school. Mark's school is having their dance next Saturday and I'm going with him. Do you think they will ask me to leave because I'm Catholic? Somehow I doubt that." She fled the room crying.

"Rose, you had better get control of her."

"Annie is right, John. Father O'Malley had no right to insult Annie. Doesn't it mean anything to you that he insulted your daughter? Where are your priorities? I'm very proud of Annie for her values and how she accepts people for who they are. I hope she has taught you something tonight."

Rose went looking for her daughter and found her sitting on Timothy's bed telling him about the disastrous evening.

"I'm not wrong. If Dad doesn't quit the country club then he is just as bad as the rest of them."

"It will be okay, Annie. Don't judge Dad. He lives in his own world of work, horses and the church. He doesn't have much else. Now go make some tea. Mom will sit me up and we will have a cup before you go to bed, and by the way, there is something good that happened tonight. Kate called and she is coming home tomorrow. She has an interview at the hospital."

CHAPTER 18

Annie paced back and forth in the airport waiting for her sister's flight. Finally the plane arrived and she spotted Kate coming down the steps and walking across the tarmac. She ran to her and hugged her tightly and didn't want to let go.

"I'm glad you're home, Kate, I have to tell you something."

"Okay, let's get my luggage and we can talk on the way home." Kate drove, as it was apparent Annie was upset.

"What's on your mind, Annie? Why do you have such a worried look on your face?"

Annie blurted out that she thought their father had a girlfriend. "I've seen him with the same woman a couple of times and they seem more than just friendly and that worries me. I talked to Sister Catherine about it and she said it was just my imagination but I don't think so, and on top of that I'm more worried about Timothy. He is not getting better. My world would fall apart if anything happens to him."

Kate set her sister's concerns about their father aside and instead said, "Annie, Timothy isn't going to get better. He is very sick and we may only have him for a few years or maybe only months. It is very sad but there is nothing the doctors can do. When the time comes, we will be strong and know that he will be in a better place."

"I don't believe that. I'll never believe that. He won't be in a better place. He belongs here with me."

Kate pulled into the driveway and they got her luggage into the house. The aroma of dinner met them at the door and Kate thought how nice it was to come home to a home-cooked meal. Annie called for her mother and Rose soon appeared in the kitchen. She hugged Kate and welcomed her back.

"I was just checking on Timothy. He was falling asleep in his chair so I have put him in bed. You can see him in the morning."

She poured them a glass of wine and while Annie set the table Rose and Kate went out to the terrace to catch up.

"How bad is Timothy, Mom? Your letters don't say too much but I think things are worse than what you write."

"I didn't want to worry you, Kate, but you're right. He is failing fast. I've done all that I can and now it's just a matter of keeping him comfortable. I'm just taking one day at a time and giving thanks for every day that I have him. I worry about Annie though. She seems to be in complete denial of his condition."

"Yes, she told me she was worried about him and she also mentioned that she is worried about Dad. How is he? I thought he would be here when I got home."

"He has been working a lot of hours but is normally here for dinner and to attend to Timothy. Unfortunately, he has a dinner meeting tonight and is sorry he won't be home until late."

Early the next morning Kate left for her interview at the hospital and was very confident she would get the internship. She was meeting her high school friend Christine for lunch. It had been a while since they had seen each other and there was a lot of catching up to do. Kate knew the conversation would revolve around Christine's infant daughter, which would take her mind off her worries.

Early into the visit Christine asked Kate if there was a special man in her life.

"I have been seeing a fellow medical student but it's nothing too serious. He plans to be a surgeon."

"Sounds like he would be quite a catch, but then again so would you."

Kate laughed. "I didn't go to medical school to catch a husband. He's a great guy but marriage is not in the cards for me at this time. I have much more to do before I ever settle down."

"Speaking of marriage," Christine said, "how are your parents?"

"Oh, they're fine. I haven't seen Dad yet. He was at a meeting last night and I went to bed before he got home. I'll see him tonight," she said nonchalantly.

When Kate arrived home her father was waiting for her. "How is our future doctor?" he said as he put his arm around her. "It's wonderful that you have done so well and I understand you'll be doing an internship at the General when you graduate. It will be good to have you home. I'm very proud of you."

Kate's thoughts flashed back to the day she told him she wanted to study medicine. He was adamantly against it, saying she could be a nurse, and now that she was almost finished he was proud of her. Thank God Mom stood by me and fought for me, she thought.

The telephone was ringing and he quickly reached for it. After a few brief words he hung up and said he had to go to the stables as one of the horses wasn't well.

"Well, I'll come along. I may not be a horse doctor but I may be able to contribute something."

"That's not necessary, Kate. The vet is meeting me there. You stay here and spend the time with your mother."

When he left she reached for Annie's car keys on the kitchen counter. She followed him carefully for several miles until he made a left-hand turn into the driveway of a beautiful Cape Cod cottage. She parked under some trees out of sight just as the door opened and a tall, dark-haired woman reached up and kissed him. She watched as they entered the cottage together.

She couldn't move. She just sat there thinking of her conversation with Annie and how her friend Christine had asked about her parents. Deep down she wondered if she already knew that her father was having an affair but was in as much denial as Annie was of Timothy. How she wanted to go and pound on the door of that cottage and demand answers from her father. But instead she pounded on the steering wheel, turned the car around and went home. Her heart was breaking, not for her, but for her mother. How could he do this to her?

Rose was reading to Timothy and Joey when Kate got home. Joey was almost asleep and Kate picked him up and carried him to bed. She then carried Timothy to bed while her mother and Annie went to the kitchen and put on a pot of tea.

Blowing on her steaming cup of tea, Kate asked Annie if she had given any thought to what she would do when she finished high school. "You're almost there," she laughed. "You better think about what you want to do."

"Dad told Sister Catherine that I was going to be a teacher. I have no idea where he got that idea but I have no intentions of becoming a teacher. I am going to study law. I know he will object but we'll cross that bridge when we come to it," Annie said with confidence.

Rose and Kate laughed. "Since when did your father's objections ever stop you?"

CHAPTER 19

The final year of Kate's internship flew by and she had decided to stay on at the General Hospital. She always knew she would return to her hometown because she felt that's where she belonged. She also knew that Timothy would not be with them much longer and her mother and Annie were going to need her strength.

There was another reason. She had been seeing Tom Gallagher, a paediatrician, and she was falling in love with him. He was a kind, compassionate man with a great sense of humor who had pulled her out of her doldrums on many occasions and she was anxious for her parents to meet him. It was arranged that they would meet at the club for dinner on Thursday night. It would not be a long evening because she and Tom had to be at the hospital early the following morning. She was hoping they could meet on Saturday night but the horses would be racing and her father would not be available. He had his priorities.

It was a very pleasant evening with everyone on their best behavior. Kate was happy that her parents immediately liked Tom. The conversation was polite and centered around the hospital but soon switched to the horses. Her father invited Tom to attend the races on Saturday with him.

"Perhaps we can make it a family affair," he said. He turned to his wife and reminded her that she hadn't been to the races at all this season. It was agreed they would attend the races and have a late dinner afterward.

The evening was turning out better than Kate expected. "That will be very nice, Dad," she said. "I'll arrange to have a nurse stay with Timothy so Annie and Joey can join us."

"Great idea, Kate. I haven't seen too much of Annie. She is so busy with her dancing and spends all her spare time with Timothy. She'll soon be finished school and then off to St. Mary's."

The waiter came to their table and asked if they would like anything else. John ordered cognac for them and signed the bill. Kate wondered just how long it had been since he talked with Annie.

She took a sip of her cognac and said, "Annie doesn't plan on going to St. Mary's. She is going to apply at the University of Toronto and wants to study law. I thought you knew."

"Well, this is all news to me," he said smiling but clearly irritated.

Rose didn't like his tone of voice or that the conversation had taken this turn. "I think it's time to call it a night. Annie is watching Timothy and Joey, and I don't want to be late getting home," she said as she pushed back her chair and stood up.

They returned to the house and Annie met them at the door in a state of panic.

"I was just about to call you at the club. Timothy is barely breathing and I can't wake him up. An ambulance is on the way. I am so scared. Help him, Kate, go help him," she cried.

Rose put her arms around Annie as Kate and Tom rushed to Timothy. Joey, sensing something was terribly wrong, clung to his father as the ambulance arrived. Kate and Tom went with Timothy and as the door of the ambulance closed Kate saw the worry on her mother's face.

It was another very close call but Timothy hung onto life. When he was stable the next morning, Kate was holding his hand when he said, "I really want to see Annie graduate."

CHAPTER 20

The summer was over and it had been a sad one for Annie. There were no more outings in the convertible, no movies and no horse races. Timothy was just too weak.

The final year of school for Annie would be starting in two weeks and she should have been looking forward to it but she was unhappy because Mark was leaving for university.

He made dinner reservations for them at his father's club the night before he was to leave. After they were seated and their dinner order had been taken, he took Annie's hand in his and placed a blue velvet box in front of her.

She opened the box to reveal a gold ring with an emerald in the center of the band. "A and M" had been engraved on the inside of the band.

"It's a promise ring, Annie," he said as he slipped the ring on her finger. "I promise to always be there for you."

She leaned across the table and kissed him. "And I promise to always be there for you, Mark. I am really going to miss you."

"The time will go by quickly, and I'll be back for the holidays. And before you know it, you'll be at university studying law."

They talked more about the future together and Mark told her that his goal, although a long way down the road, was to open a law practice with his father. Annie laughed and said that when she graduated from law school, although a longer road for her, she would join them.

CHAPTER 21

"Well, Annie, we are coming into the home stretch and I am so proud of how well you have done this year. Final exams start next week and if you need any help or have any questions, I am here for you."

Home stretch? thought Annie. That's a racing term. What could Sister Catherine possibly know about horse racing?

Over the next two weeks Annie rarely surfaced from studying and working on her Dr. Tom Dooley essay, which would be entered in the English competition. The winner would receive five hundred dollars, but more important than the money, it would look good on her application to the university. The students had been given a list of universities and their requirements but Annie knew where she wanted to go.

Annie was a lot calmer than expected in the last week of finals. She had done all that she could do and her attitude seemed to be "let the chips fall where they may." She was done with the books and now she just wanted to concentrate on the convocation and prom.

She designed her dress with her mother's help and it was being made by the best seamstress in town. When she tried on the floor-length turquoise peau de soie gown for the first time she felt like Cinderella as she swirled around the dressing room. Her parents gave her a single strand of pearls with matching earrings, and Kate's gift of a mink shoulder wrap completed the outfit.

Mark would be coming home to escort her to the dance and she could barely contain her excitement at seeing him again. All the phone calls and letters they had exchanged during the year were wonderful. She had tied the letters together with a blue ribbon and read them over and over but they could not replace the safe feeling of his arms around her.

Two weeks before the prom, there was an announcement on the bulletin board that the final marks would be handed out in the office at one o'clock. Annie stood in line and when she heard her name she stepped forward and received her marks. The bright red stamp on the right hand corner said, "Graduated with Honors," and she had placed second in the class. She lowered her head and breathed a sigh of relief. All the long nights of study, the sleepless nights, the worry and the encouragement from Timothy washed over her.

After all the marks had been handed out, Sister Catherine announced that Annie O'Brien had won the English essay competition. The class clapped and congratulated her but they were really waiting to hear who would be valedictorian.

The nun stood tall as she told the class that the board had chosen Annie O'Brien to be their valedictorian. The room went silent and Annie gasped audibly. Everyone was shocked that it wasn't Janet Lewis. Class was dismissed but Annie stayed behind.

The kindly nun put her arm around her. "Your father is going to be so proud."

Annie backed away. "I can't accept this. Janet Lewis should be valedictorian. She has been an honor student throughout high school."

"You can't refuse, and why would you?" the exasperated nun said with a raised voice. "You have no idea of the sacrifices I have made for you. How I have tried to protect you and the amount of time I have spent with you. You are a very ungrateful person. Your father will be furious with you." She paced the floor, rolling up the long black sleeves of her habit, and tucked her hands under the starched bib.

"My father has nothing to do with this, and if by helping me you feel I owe you then you did it for the wrong reasons. And what did you have to protect me from? You ask me why I refuse this honor and I ask why I was given it."

The nun sank into her chair and closed her eyes.

"You don't understand, Annie. Janet is a Protestant, she can't be valedictorian."

With those words, Annie thought she was going to be sick. She backed away further. "This is wrong and you know it. You have to make it right."

CHAPTER 22

Annie woke to the sun shining through her window and listened to the birds singing as she tiptoed toward Timothy's room. The door was slightly ajar so she peeked in and found he was still asleep.

The aroma of bacon and pancakes took her downstairs where she found her mother and father having breakfast with Kate and Joey.

"I thought you would be up at the crack of dawn," her mother said, smiling. "This is your big day, Annie." She set a place for her daughter and served her breakfast.

"I'm not hungry, Mom. I'd just like tea and toast. I have butterflies in my stomach."

"You should have more than that. This is going to be a long day for you," her father said as he topped up her tea.

Annie took a sip of her tea. "It would be perfect if Timothy could come. Are you sure he is not well enough, Kate. He wouldn't have to stay for the whole ceremony."

Kate reached across and rubbed her sister's back. Her look told Annie what she didn't want to hear.

"You better get ready," Kate said. "According to the program you brought home, you have to be at the auditorium by eleven o'clock for the class picture. I'll drive you when you're ready, and don't forget your cap and gown."

Timothy woke as they were leaving and Annie ran upstairs to say goodbye. "Next time I see you I'll be a graduate and I'll tell you every little detail."

"Good luck, Annie," he said sleepily.

Sister Catherine was wringing her hands as Annie entered the school with her cap and gown over her arm.

"Where have you been? We've been waiting for you. You're the last one to arrive. Now hurry and get into your position," the nun said as she directed Annie to her place and the class picture was taken.

After a graduate luncheon hosted by the nuns, the students were ready for the processional march into the auditorium. As she made her way down the aisle, Annie spotted her family and they gave her a little wave.

Sister Catherine stood at the podium and welcomed the parents and guests and introduced Janet Lewis, who would deliver the valedictory.

Father O'Reilly handed out the diplomas along with a single white rose to each graduate. The whole ceremony was over in an hour and Annie went looking for her parents amid the crowd outside in the garden where afternoon tea was being served.

She spotted them talking to Father O'Reilly and as she approached them they clapped and shouted "Bravo!" Annie was grinning from ear to ear as she showed off her diploma.

"Well, congratulations, Annie, you made it and on the Honor Roll," said Father O'Reilly. "Now it's off to St. Mary's University where I know you will do well. They have a great Education Faculty."

"I'm not going to St. Mary's," was all Annie said.

"Don't be preposterous, Annie, of course you're going to St. Mary's," her father said with a little laugh.

"You were right, Mom, this has been a long day. I'm tired and anxious to go home and show Timothy my diploma. Can we leave now?"

Everyone said their goodbyes, shaking hands and smiling. Annie could hardly wait to leave.

When they arrived home she burst through the front door, throwing her cap and gown aside. Rose and Kate followed her.

"We're back, Timothy. Look at my diploma. I'm going to hang it in your room."

The nurse who had been staying with Timothy was standing by his bed and Annie shook him and told him to wake up. He took a tiny breath and smiled. "What's all the commotion about?" he asked.

Kate took his hand and discreetly took his pulse. She wondered how much pain he was having, but thought that they would never know because Timothy never complained. She straightened out his weakened body, adjusted the bed and fluffed up the pillows.

"Are you comfortable, Timothy?" she asked.

"I'm fine, thanks, Kate. Now I want to hear all about Annie's day."

Annie stood at the foot of her brother's bed with tears running down her face. She wanted to hug him, tell him how much she loved him, how she would never have made it without him by her side, but she stood there silently and realized for the first time that the day would come when he would no longer be by her side.

"Why the tears, Annie? You should be dancing around with joy," Timothy said. "You are now a graduate and will soon be off to university before you know it."

"I'm just happy that it's all over, but I will be a lot happier when I get an acceptance letter from the university. How much longer will it take? Do you think I'll get accepted?"

"I have no doubt you will get accepted. Now stop worrying about the letter because there is nothing you can do about it. Just think about the prom tonight. What time is Mark picking you up?"

"He'll be here at seven o'clock sharp and I suggested to him an orchid corsage would be nice. I don't want carnations or roses; they are so pedestrian. I want something different."

"You are definitely different, my Annie. I'd like to rest now, come and get me when dinner is ready."

She slid off the bed, kissed him and quietly left the room.

CHAPTER 23

She heard the letter slot in the door open as the mail fell to the floor. The letter on top had the words "University of Toronto, Admissions Office," on the upper left-hand side. Her hand was shaking as she picked up the letter that she had been anxiously waiting for and went to Timothy.

"It's here. The letter from the university is here and I'm afraid to open it. What if I haven't been accepted?"

"You'll never know until you open it, Annie. Open it now. I can't bear the suspense," he said with a smile, never doubting for a moment she wouldn't be accepted.

She tore at the envelope and gasped, "I'm in! I'm in." She hollered for her mother, who came running, fearing Timothy had taken a bad turn. With great relief she hugged her daughter.

"I'm so proud of you." All three of them were crying and laughing at the same time.

"When does she have to leave, Mom?" Timothy asked.

"In three weeks, which doesn't give us a lot of time but we will have her ready to go."

At dinner that evening the big announcement was made. John looked over at his daughter and then at his wife.

"Are you sure this is what you want to do, Annie?" he asked. "Toronto is a long way from home and you'll get homesick."

"I'll be fine, Dad."

He knew there was no sense in arguing with her. Once she made up her mind there was no stopping her.

The next few weeks were spent shopping, attending farewell parties and spending as much time as she could with Mark. The night before she left they had dinner together and Annie gave him her class ring, which fit his small finger perfectly. It was a happy evening and she didn't want it to end, but she also wanted to spend some time with Timothy.

As Mark drove her home, an ambulance rushed by them with the siren blaring.

Annie looked over at Mark with a panicked look on her face and he went full speed. As he pulled into the driveway, Rose was getting into her car with Joey.

"Come, Mrs. O'Brien, I'll drive you."

"I thank you, Mark, but I'll drive."

When they got to the hospital and found his room, two nurses were standing by Timothy's oxygen tent while Kate was consulting with his doctor. Annie watched terrified, and Mark's arm tightened around her.

"Where is Dad?" Kate asked her mother. "He should be here, Mom."

Rose took Joey home, and Mark and Annie followed, knowing there was nothing they could do. When they arrived home she telephoned the stables but there was no answer, so she left the house and drove to the stables in search of her husband. She parked her car in front of the tack room, looked around and saw his car. She stepped inside and called for him but there was no response. A clipboard was hanging from a nail to the right of the door. She took it down and flipped through John's notes, looking for a blank piece of paper. She recognized his handwriting but there was also an unfamiliar feminine script.

She hastily wrote a note that told him to come to the hospital immediately. Too worried about Timothy, she gave no more thought to the strange handwriting and returned to the hospital. She found Kate sitting alone with her head on the bed close to Timothy's. Her tears had stained the bed sheet. When she saw her mother, she stood up and said, "He's gone, Mom. He never regained consciousness."

Annie was half-asleep when she heard her mother and sister return. She jumped out of bed just as her mother opened the bedroom door and, by the look of sadness on her face, Annie knew Timothy had died. As she wrapped her arms around her mother she saw her father standing at the bedroom door.

She flew into a rage screaming that Timothy was dead and where had he been? She pounded her fists on his chest and hung onto him. Rose stared at her husband as his hand fell on her shoulder. "I'm so sorry," he said. There was no acknowledgement on Rose's part yet her shoulder moved at his touch. She wondered if he was sorry his son had died or sorry that he hadn't been there for his family.

The following morning, Father O'Reilly arrived at the house as the family was leaving for Fitzpatrick's Funeral Home. He said, "Rose, I am so sorry. I know how you must feel but he is now with his Maker and at peace."

"Thank you," she said, "but you couldn't possibly know how I feel."

They arrived at the funeral home and Mr. Fitzpatrick met them at the door. He was a quiet, regal man and his son, Mike, was a friend of Annie's. As Annie shook his hand she remembered the many times she and her friends would ask, "How's business?" and he would reply, "Dead, very dead," and they would laugh. But it was no laughing matter now.

They were escorted to the casket room and Annie saw a polished, dark mahogany casket with thick brass handles that gleamed. It was lined with white satin. "This is the one, Mom."

Father O'Reilly came into the room and Annie went over to him to ask why he was here. Before he could answer, she told him to leave. Her father stepped in and apologized for Annie. "You'll have to excuse her," he said. "It's obvious she is very upset over the death of her brother." They shook hands and the priest assured John that he would be officiating at the High Mass for Timothy.

"I want him out of here," Annie said. "He has no business being here. Don't you remember, Dad, how he wouldn't let Timothy be part of the First Communion procession? I remember."

The funeral was scheduled for Saturday at eleven o'clock and just as the family was about to leave, the telephone rang. John answered.

"I'll be there," he said. "The funeral will be over at three o'clock, which gives me time to get to the track for the first race." He hung up the phone. Annie was standing beside him.

"You are going to race your horses on the day your son is being buried? Are you crazy?" she asked.

He gave no explanation as he looked down at his daughter and realized he was losing her too, if he hadn't already.

It was the first time in years that Rose had been in a church. The Cathedral of the Holy Trinity was stately with a ceiling that seemed to reach the sky, the row upon row of candles stood guard over her son. An organist was playing a solemn hymn and the pews were filled with friends. She stood at the back of the church looking toward the front and saw a massive spray of orchids covering the top of her son's casket. She knew Mark had sent them.

With her husband at her side and the children behind them, she started the long walk down the aisle. It could have been fifty feet or a thousand feet; she knew it would be the longest walk she would ever take.

After Mass, the pallbearers carried the casket to the waiting hearse. It slowly drove away making the journey to St. Joseph's cemetery. It entered the grounds and wound around the road until it came to a stop. John took his wife's arm as they walked to their son's final resting place. Father O'Reilly stood at the grave saying prayers and anointed the casket as it was lowered into the ground. And it was over.

A luncheon was held at the Shadow Inn for their friends, but Rose pulled her husband aside and asked him to take her home. She could take no more of hearing "I'm so sorry" and "He's in a better place."

When they got home, she got out of the car as John held the door for her. She walked slowly up the walk and mounted the five steps to the front door, trying hard not to look at the wheelchair ramp. Her keys were clutched tightly in her hand; they were damp as she inserted the house key into the lock.

John stood beside her and said he had to go to the stables. His steps resounded on the walkway and the purr of the car's motor and crunch of tires assured her she was alone. She twisted the key, touching the cool wood of the door. The stillness of the house engulfed her as she went in and dropped the keys on the desk. They made a metallic sound that startled her. It reminded her of the sound of a pallbearer's ring hitting the side of her son's casket. She wept alone. Her first-born son was dead and her whole way of life was gone.

CHAPTER 24

Annie left a week after the funeral with great sadness in her heart. She didn't want to leave her mother. "I'll be fine, Annie, and I'll see you at Christmas," she was told as she boarded the airplane.

With only one child left in the house, Rose threw all her energy and time into her younger son, whom she felt had been neglected over the past few months. Joey was a good student but his first love was hockey. The coming Saturday was especially important for him, as the junior hockey awards banquet was being held at the club and, although he didn't say it, Joey was hoping for the top award.

It would be the first time Rose had been to the club since the funeral, and she wasn't looking forward to seeing everyone with their sympathetic words. But it never happened. No one mentioned Timothy, and Rose realized that life goes on and she had better get on with hers.

After the banquet luncheon the awards were being announced. Joey sat next to his mother, squeezing her hand. He wanted the Best Player trophy but when his name was announced he could barely move. Rose pushed him forward and he walked to the front of the room, everyone clapping — his mother clapping the loudest — and he accepted the golden statute with pride.

As they were leaving, he kept looking at his prize and said, "I wish Dad had been here. He would have been surprised."

Rose checked the time and said, "Let's go show him." They drove to the stables and as she parked the car she noticed the tack room door was open. She told Joey to wait in the car. She walked through the tack room into the sitting area where she found her husband sitting on the leather couch with his arm around a woman. Although it had been years since Rose had seen the woman, she recognized her immediately.

"My God, Rose, what are you doing here?" John demanded.

"Your son, Joey, came to show you his hockey trophy. You do remember you have another son, don't you? But it's obvious you're busy, although I do suggest you take a minute and come outside to congratulate him."

When they got home Joey called Kate and told her about his win, and as he hung up he heard his father's car. He took the stairs two at a time and met his father at the door with his trophy in hand. John joined in his son's excitement and told him how proud he was. Several of Joey's friends were at the door and they raced upstairs taking turns holding the prize. "Mom's in the living room," Joey hollered back to his father.

John took off his jacket and sat in an easy chair across from his wife.

"We need to talk, Rose," he started. "I'm sorry you had to find out about Terry this way. I didn't mean for this to happen but she was the only one I could talk to when Timothy was failing and one thing just led to another. If you had been there for me, this would never have happened. I loved you."

"Don't do a guilt transfer with me, John. I just want to know where we go from here. What are your plans?"

"I don't have any plans. Things can remain as they are. Why should they change? You have everything you need and want. We will just carry on as we always have."

"Don't be so naive. It would be best if you moved your things out. I will decide what I have to do." The doorbell was ringing and Rose thought it was more of Joey's friends but when she opened the door Kate and Tom were standing there with grins as wide as a full moon.

"We came to see the great winner and his trophy and we have some news of our own. We're getting married and have set the date for December 22."

John didn't move out, and for the next several months the house hummed with wedding plans. Annie arrived home a week before the wedding, filled with her stories of university life, and Mark was also home for the Christmas holidays.

The day of the wedding was clear with a light snow falling as the bride entered the church on her father's arm in a stunning short, white velvet dress carrying a cascade of stargazer lilies. Annie led them down the aisle wearing a short red velvet dress and carried white orchids. Father O'Reilly married the happy couple and the reception was held at the club.

As the guests filed along the receiving line they gushed with compliments on what a perfect couple Kate and Tom made, how Annie had grown, how hard it was to believe she was in law school, how tall Joey was becoming. The O'Briens stood together unified — the picture of the perfect family.

A month after the wedding, Rose consulted with Laura Parks, a young lawyer who had just opened her practice and who didn't know John. At their first meeting, she asked Rose if she was having an affair. Rose was shocked. "Of course not, my husband is and that's why I want a divorce."

Within a week the papers were filed and John was served.

She heard the slam of his car door and braced herself. He came through the door, papers in hand and threw them in her face, demanding to know if she was in her right mind.

"I won't ever give you a divorce!" he yelled. "Why can't you leave things just as they are? Look around. Do you want to give up this high standard of living? You just don't get it."

"I get the fact that you're having an affair with Theresa Williams, a former nun, the teacher who taught your daughter. How are you going to explain that to Annie? I felt for a long time that you were being unfaithful to me. When I went to see Father O'Reilly about a scholarship for Kate, I indicated to him that I knew what was going on. He thought I knew at that time it was Theresa but I didn't. That's the only reason Kate was granted the scholarship despite you being against it. There's nothing more to be said, John. Have your lawyer contact mine and let's just get this done."

He paced back and forth, jiggling the keys in his pocket.

"I want you to go now and leave your house key on the desk on your way out."

He left without another word but he didn't leave his key.

The following day she had the locks changed, packed his clothes and sent them to the stables. She was on a mission.

The next thing on her list was to tell her children. She called Kate and asked her to drop over with Tom when she got off work. She wasn't too concerned about them but she was worried about how Joey would react. He was only ten years old. Would he understand?

She was making tea with Joey when they arrived. "What's going on, Mom? You sounded so serious on the phone."

Kate took her time and poured the tea.

"There is no soft way to give you this news. I am divorcing your father."

Kate didn't seem visibly upset but Joey was very confused. "Why do you want to divorce Dad? Don't you love him anymore? Doesn't he love us? What are we going to do? Do we have to move? Is this my fault?"

Rose pulled her son down next to her and assured him he had done nothing wrong and his father loved him. "Everything is going to be okay. You are not to worry."

He said, "Alright," and went to his room but Rose knew his world had just been turned upside down.

Kate went and sat by her mother.

"When did all this take place, Mom? What does Dad have to say about it, and why?"

"Your father has been having an affair with a woman for many years. I had my suspicions but did nothing about it because of Timothy but now that he is no longer with us, this is something I have to do, as much as it is going to hurt everyone. You and Annie are old enough to accept this but my main concern is Joey. Annie will be home tomorrow for the summer and I'll break the news to her then."

Rose was at the airport the next morning waiting for her daughter. Annie came through the gate with a big smile and flew into her mother's arms. "I'm so happy to be home, Mom, even if it is just for a short while."

On the ride home Annie kept up a constant chatter about her new friends, and how her grades were better than she had ever expected. "I love the law," she exclaimed, "and I love the fact that Mark is also home, too." She also said she wanted to see Sister Catherine. They had stayed in touch with letters and she had been so encouraging.

"Life is good, Mom," she said as they arrived home.

When Annie had settled in, she found her mother sitting at the kitchen table with a fresh pot of tea. Rose had always found comfort in tea and she hoped it would get her through what she had to tell her daughter.

"Please sit down, Annie. Things have changed since you've been away and the biggest change is that I'm divorcing your father. I want you to understand that my reason has nothing to do with you or anyone else. This is between your father and me."

Annie put down her teacup and looked straight into her mother's eyes. "I'm not surprised, Mom. Dad seems to have a life of his own and I've thought that for a long time."

Rose was completely surprised at her reaction and at a loss for words.

"Do you think that he has a girlfriend and is that why you're divorcing him?"

"Yes, he does." Rose knew what the next question would be and wondered if she should tell Annie. She had never lied to her daughter before, why start now?

"Who is she?"

"Her nickname is Terry but you would know her as Sister Theresa."

Annie thought for a moment, her mind confused. Her mouth opened wide.

"Oh, my God," she said in wonder. "You don't mean that awful nun who was so hateful to me. Dad has obviously lost his mind. Where is he? When will he be home? I've got to talk to him."

"Your father has moved out of the house and I understand he is living with Terry."

"Mom, I'm so sorry this has happened. I have an appointment to see Sister Catherine this evening. Would it be okay if I talked to her about this?"

Rose didn't reply. She knew Annie would talk to her trusted friend and she also knew if Sister Catherine was honest with Annie, her daughter was in for another shock.

Annie arrived at the Sacred Heart Convent earlier than expected. A young novice answered the door and silently guided Annie to the reception area. She waited only a few minutes before Sister Catherine came into the room. After the greetings and hugs, they went to the chesterfield where tea was waiting on the side table.

"I have some terrible news to tell you, Sister, and you are going to be so surprised," Annie started.

Sister Catherine reached for Annie's hand, fearing that what was coming was not going to be pleasant and hoping the news she had to tell her would not shatter their friendship.

"Dad is having an affair with a woman who used to be a nun and Mom is divorcing him. This woman taught me when I went to St. Peter's Girls School and she was so mean to me. I just can't believe it. You must know her. It's Sister Theresa."

The nun sat very still, holding the crucifix attached to her habit, and said a silent prayer.

"I do know her, Annie, and I know about the divorce. It is very sad, and even sadder because Sister Theresa is my biological sister. When she told me she was still In love with your father, I tried to talk sense into her but she wouldn't listen to me. She entered the convent two years after I did and I didn't think at the time that she would make it because she entered for the wrong reasons. She was your father's high school sweetheart and everyone thought they would marry, but your father met your mother and when they married, Theresa's heart was broken."

"What do you mean? What are you saying?" Annie cried. "Have you known all this time about the affair? Is that why you befriended me because of your guilt? If that's the case, then all the years I have known you our friendship has been nothing more than a lie. You are not a friend, you deceived me and I will never forgive you."

Tears were starting to well in her eyes but she was determined the nun would not see her cry. She picked up her car keys and purse and, with her head held high, she left the convent, never to go back again.

Annie returned home to the open arms of her mother and sobbed until she was exhausted. Her mother held her and told her over and over that they would get through this together.

CHAPTER 25

Rose got her divorce and full custody of Joey but little else. She could remain in the house until Joey was of age and John would cover the household expenses. She would receive three hundred dollars a week for Joey, but nothing for herself and John would only pay fifty percent of Annie's school expenses. At the final meeting with the lawyers, John told her that she had her divorce but she would never make it without him.

"We'll see," Rose thought to herself. She would take one step at a time. The first step would be to get a job. She applied at the art gallery where she had worked when she was Annie's age and was hired immediately on a part-time basis. Her pay was a hundred dollars a week. This would help, although there wouldn't be enough money for Annie's education. For the first time in years she worried about money. John had always taken care of all the bills and he would give her an allowance of fifty dollars a week — mad money he called it. Well, she needed more than mad money now.

Annie sat hunched over the classified ads of the local newspaper, pencil in hand, with Joey sitting beside her while Rose was preparing dinner.

"What are you looking for, Annie?" he asked.

"I'm going to get a summer job and this one sounds pretty good. The radio station is looking for a receptionist for summer relief and they're paying fifty dollars a week. I'm going to apply and I'll get it. Where's the adding machine, Mom? I'm going to figure out just how much money I will make."

Joey agreed that she would definitely get the job, while Rose shook her head and smiled.

The following day Annie appeared at the station and found ten other girls applying for the job. During the interview the station manager asked if she was John O'Brien's daughter.

"Yes, I am."

"Well, I know your father very well and if you want the job, it's yours."

Annie didn't care if she was hired because of her father. She just wanted the job. She would bank all the money she earned from her summer job and knew it would help with her school. She planned to get a part-time job when she got to university and convinced herself she could work and keep up with her studies.

It was a short summer. With her job there wasn't much time for socializing but she did spend as much time as possible with Mark. He was her shoulder to lean on and he listened without judgment as she told him about her father's affair, the divorce and her friend's betrayal. They talked about future plans and how they wanted to be together, but first they must get their degrees. It was a long way off but they had lots of time.

CHAPTER 26

When Annie got back to Toronto, the first thing she did was buy the daily paper and search out the help wanted ads. One ad in particular jumped out at her.

"WANTED: Dancers. Paying up to two hundred dollars a show. Auditions at the Chatelaine Club, 9002 Bloor Lane, 9:00 pm, September 15."

The address of the audition was not in a familiar section of the city but Annie eventually found it. She stared up at the neon sign and had second thoughts about auditioning.

WELCOME TO THE CHATELAINE CLUB — A GENTLEMAN'S CLUB

A well-dressed man came over to her car and asked if she was there for the audition. She picked up her dance bag and followed him into the club. He led her to an office where eight other girls were waiting.

"Take a seat. The boss will be here in a minute," he said.

Annie took a seat next to a pretty redhead. "What's your name?" she asked.

"Annie O'Brien."

"Oh God, girl, we don't use our real names in this business. What's your stage name? I'm Paradise."

"I don't have a stage name," Annie said nervously and thought perhaps this wasn't the place for her.

"Well, you better think of one before the boss gets here. Humm... You look pretty fragile and innocent. I think Orchid would be a good name for you. Yeah, tell him your name is Orchid."

Annie thought of Mark and the orchid corsage he gave her on prom night and the orchids that covered Timothy's casket.

The boss strutted in wearing cowboy boots and an open-neck shirt revealing six gold chains. He surveyed the nine girls and said, "Okay, get into your costumes and make it snappy. I'll be back in fifteen minutes."

They went to the Dressing Room and eight girls scampered around, opening their bags, pulling out wigs, makeup and stiletto heels. Annie sat there not knowing what to do. What she brought certainly wasn't what she needed. She got up to leave.

"Where are you going, Orchid? Hurry, we only have fifteen minutes and he'll be back," Paradise said as she pulled on her wig.

"I don't have anything," Annie said.

"Well, c'mon over here, between all of us we can find something for you. Hurry."

When she finished dressing she didn't recognize herself in the mirror. She was wearing a long, curly blonde wig that itched her head, false eyelashes, blue glittery eye shadow, a red beaded bra with matching short shorts and Paradise had tied a black lace wrap around her hips.

Paradise lit two cigarettes and handed one to Annie.

"Thanks, Paradise, but I don't smoke." A dancer hearing this reached over and took the second cigarette.

"You look great," Paradise said. "He's gonna love ya. You have an innocent look about you, a baby face. You're gonna make a lot of money and you have great legs. Are you going to be able to dance in those stilettos? I'll bet you have never stripped before, have you?"

Annie admitted she hadn't.

"Don't worry. I'll show you the ropes. I've been stripping for five years and have made a ton of money, and you will too. This is a good club, the best in town. The customers aren't allowed to touch you but they will try. Just tip the bouncers ten bucks and they will watch out for you.

Exactly fifteen minutes later the boss walked into the Dressing Room. He looked the girls over and said he would only be hiring one as he led them to the stage. One by one the girls went on stage and did their routine.

Annie thought it wasn't really dancing. The girls just sort of walked around the stage, not even to the beat of the music, twirled around a brass pole and that was it. She could do that.

It was her turn to perform.

She stepped up onto the stage and as the music began she started to sway to the rhythm. The lights were on her, and the boss and the other girls were watching as she flowed from one end of the stage to the other. She was in her own world. The music stopped.

Silence. Then clapping hands started. She looked over at Paradise, who was clapping the loudest and smiled up at Annie. The boss was even clapping.

"You're great. You're hired. The rest of you can go home," he said. "We have our new dancer."

He turned and walked away.

"Oh, no," Annie said. "I can't stay if Paradise can't work here. We're a team and we dance together. I'm sorry but I can't work here without Paradise."

The girls started to head back to the Dressing Room.

"Alright, alright. She can stay. Oh, what the hell, all of you can stay. Yeah, yeah, I know. The girls that dance together stay together."

Annie felt a little stab in her heart as she recalled Bishop Fulton Sheen's words: "The family that prays together stays together."

"Be here Friday night at nine sharp. The doors open at ten and the guys will be lined up. Be ready. There will be a House Mom here and she'll go over all the rules with you. I'm assuming you are all twenty-one years old." He looked directly at Annie but she said nothing.

Back in the Dressing Room the girls gathered around Annie and thanked her. "We're here for you, Orchid. Anything you want or need, just let us know."

Paradise walked Annie to her car.

"I'll see you Friday night, Orchid. Come at eight o'clock and I'll show you how to put on makeup and get dressed. Don't go buying stuff. I've got everything you'll need. I owe you, my little friend. I've been wanting to dance at this club for months. Had several auditions but never got lucky until tonight." She closed Annie's car door and disappeared into the night.

On the drive back to the dorm all Annie could think of was the money. Her mother would never have to worry about her education and she would never find out how she made the money. They lived in two different cities, miles apart.

CHAPTER 27

The following Friday, Annie arrived at the club and looked around for Paradise. She started to walk across the Dressing Room in search of her when a voice from behind stopped her.

"Are you one of the new girls?" a matronly woman asked.

"Yes," replied Annie. "This is my first night and I'm looking for Paradise, another new girl."

"She isn't here yet. I'm the House Mom. My name is Marty. Before you get dressed there are rules I have to go over with you. First and most important the customers are not allowed to touch you. We don't do lap dances here. You just stand in front of the guy and do your thing. This is just a topless club so only the top comes off. When dancing onstage you will do two numbers, one with your top on and the other with the top off. You work four hours and get paid two hundred dollars cash at the end of your shift. Any tips you make from the customers are yours to keep, but you must tip the DJ, the bouncers and me. Tip whatever you want but the more you tip the more the guys will take care of you. Don't get involved with anyone who works here. It's the fastest way to lose your job. If it's a choice between a bouncer and a dancer, the dancer is always the one to go. Dancers are a dime a dozen. Any questions?"

Annie said no, she had no questions. It was after eight o'clock and no sign of Paradise. What in the world would she do? She brought nothing, believing Paradise would keep her word. The clock was ticking. Annie broke out into a cold sweat as the Dressing Room door swung open and in flew Paradise.

"Orchid, I'm so sorry I'm late. I stopped at the DJ booth and asked Harold about tonight's schedule. You will be the third dancer on stage so that gives me time to get you ready. Come over here and let's get started. I'm so sorry I'm late. I can tell by your eyes that you were worried. Okay, let's start from the bottom up, here's a couple of G-strings."

She handed Annie a satin, royal blue strip of fabric, which Annie felt didn't leave much to the imagination. She slipped it over her long legs and put on a pair of royal blue short shorts with a matching sequined bra.

While Annie was getting dressed, Paradise went to the bar and came back with a couple of drinks.

"Come over here under the makeup light. Sit down and close your eyes," Paradise said as she took a sip of her drink. "You won't recognize yourself when I'm finished."

She slipped a short, curly blonde wig on her. "I picked this wig for you, Orchid, because it has a jazzy look to it. It suits you," she said while adjusting the curls.

Next came the pancake makeup, blue eye shadow, pink rouge on her cheeks and pink lipstick.

"Okay, Orchid, we're just about done. I'm glad we wear the same size shoes. Try these on; they are my favorites, not quite as high as the other stilettos."

Annie slipped the silver stilettos on, stood up, looked in the mirror and gasped.

"Is that really me?" she said.

"You bet it is, and you look smashing. Now practise walking around. You need to learn the stripper walk. Put a hand on your hip, as you take a step cross one foot over the other and drag the other foot around. Hold your head high and smile. Now try it."

Annie did as she was told. She was a natural. Sashaying across the floor, Paradise hollered, "You've got it, Orchid, you've got it, swing those hips and smile."

The DJ was announcing that Orchid was the next dancer on stage.

"Oh, my goodness, it's my turn to go on stage, Paradise, can I do it?" she cried.

"Of course you can, now get going. They're waiting for you. Hold your head high and smile, smile, smile. Go on, I have to finish getting ready," Paradise said as she pushed Annie through the Dressing Room door toward the stage.

Annie climbed the few steps to center stage, grabbed the brass pole and started her dance. The club was dark, just the lights were on Annie as she lifted her leg and wrapped it around the pole bending backwards. The men shouted and cheered.

"Take it off!" they shouted. "Take it off."

Annie looked down at the men sitting around the stage. They were throwing dollar bills at her feet, but she kicked them aside and smiled, so they started tossing five-dollar bills. She continued dancing to the first song. The lights dimmed and her second dance started.

Paradise was watching from the corner. "Take off your top, Orchid, take off your top," she whispered to herself. But Annie didn't. The men were now screaming, "Take it off, take it off!"

As the last bars of the song were being played, Annie reached behind her, undid the bra hook, turned her back to the men and with the bra around her index finger she twirled it in the air as the music ended and the lights went down. In a split second she had the bra back on. She stood there smiling as the crowd roared.

Jeff, the bouncer, helped her pick up the money on the stage.

"I'll get this for you, Orchid," he said. "You're beautiful, and you sure pulled a fast one on these guys. They loved it. Paradise is up next, so get off the stage and I'll bring this cash to you."

As Annie was heading to the Dressing Room, a customer stopped her and asked for a private dance.

"I'll be right back," she said.

Jeff followed her into the Dressing Room and they counted her stage money. There was a total of seventy-five dollars.

"Oh, yeah, they really like you."

Annie thanked him and handed him twenty dollars.

"I'll watch over you like a hawk, Orchid, you're different, not like the others. Anyone gives you trouble, I'll be right there. Now freshen up the lipstick and I'll take you to the customer who is waiting for you. He's a regular with a lot of money and you must have impressed him good because he rarely asks for a private dance."

The customer didn't want a private dance after all. He just wanted to sit and talk. He started by asking Annie a lot of questions about herself but she quickly switched the conversation back to him. She learned he was married with three children, a surgeon at the General Hospital. He came to the club on Friday nights to relax and have a drink and hoped Annie would be there next week. She assured him she would be. He got up to leave and handed her some folded money. Never once did he attempt to touch her.

Paradise was fixing her makeup as Annie entered the Dressing Room.

"How did you do, Orchid? That guy comes in here every Friday and he's a big tipper."

Annie opened her hand and looked at the folded money. She counted five one-hundred-dollar bills and started to tell Paradise but Paradise stopped her.

"I don't want to know how much money you made. Don't tell anyone. That's your business. There is a lot of competition here and the other dancers can make your life miserable. Put your money in your locker and make sure it's locked up tight. If they can steal it from you, they will."

"We just have another hour to work. Do you want to get something to eat when we finish?"

Annie hesitated. She thought of the assignments she needed to have ready for Monday. She was very tired and as much as she liked Paradise she didn't think it was a good idea to become too friendly. It would be best to remain club friends only.

"I'll take a rain check, if that's okay. I'm really tired and tomorrow I want to shop for a few outfits. I can't thank you enough for all that you have done for me."

"No problem. I'll see you tomorrow night. Don't forget to tip the House Mom."

CHAPTER 28

The Christmas season was approaching and Annie told the club she would not be available over the holidays. She would be on vacation for the month of December.

"You can't have the time off, Orchid," the boss said. "Christmas is a busy time for us and we need you here."

"Sorry, boss, but that is impossible."

Final exams were around the corner and Annie had a lot of catching up to do. She had worked very hard between her studies and the dancing, so far managing to stay on the honors list, and she wanted to keep it that way. There was also Christmas shopping to be done before going home for the holidays. She had a lot on her mind but the one thing that worried her constantly was her mother. During her weekly telephone calls home her mother had lost the smile in her voice and Annie knew she wasn't happy. She didn't plan on telling her she was coming home for Christmas; she was just going to show up.

"Orchid, the Doctor is in the house. Are you ready? You're next on stage." Jeff said as he tapped her on the shoulder and her thoughts snapped back to reality.

Annie was dressed in a short yellow sequined dress, which showed off her legs. She slipped on gold stilettos, checked her false eyelashes and brushed a bit of gold glitter on her cheeks. Paradise nodded her approval by lifting her eyebrows and smiling.

Annie stepped up onto the stage and did her routine. When it came time for her to take down the top of her dress, she coyly slid the thin strap off her shoulder and the lights faded.

"Hey, that's not what I came for," one of the men hollered.

"Well, that's all you're gettin'," Jeff hammered back as he gathered up Orchid's tips and led her to the Doctor.

"You are beautiful, Orchid," the Doctor said as he took her hand and poured her a glass of champagne. "I was wondering if you would be interested in going away with me for a few days before Christmas. The rainy, cloudy weather is miserable and I thought you might like to get away to the sun and rest up before the holidays."

Warm sunny days, ocean breezes, white sand and lots of rest with no worries — what a wonderful thought — but Annie knew that would never happen.

She smiled and thanked him but told him she had plans for Christmas and would only be dancing for one more week until after the holidays. He voiced his disappointment, saying, "Perhaps another time," and suggested that they could have dinner together. Annie picked up her champagne glass, held it to her lips and just smiled. She had no intention of ever having dinner with him; all she wanted was his money. He stayed for a few hours, talking about himself, and handed her folded bills when he left, wishing her a Merry Christmas as he leaned over and kissed her on the cheek. Back in the Dressing Room she counted a thousand dollars, and Jeff had picked up two hundred from her stage. Not a bad night. She mentally counted the money she had saved and calculated that there was more than enough to finish her year at school and for her trip home.

CHAPTER 29

The snow was piling up and the wind whistled through the trees as Annie parked her rental car beside the darkened house. She opened the door with her key and called to her mother. There was no reply. She walked through the house, turning on the lights. A fire was slowly dying in the fireplace, she threw on another log and got it roaring again. She found her mother upstairs asleep on her bed. The tear-stained pillow told Annie just how sad her mother was. She looked down at her and was shocked at how thin she had become. Her hair had lost its shine and she was very pale.

"Mom, it's me," Annie said as she gently shook her mother's shoulder.

Rose sat up and, without a word, hugged her daughter and sobbed. She didn't ask how or why Annie was home; she was just happy she was holding her.

"Where is Joey?" Annie asked.

"He's having Christmas Eve dinner with his father and should be home very soon," Rose said as she ran her fingers through her hair and looked at the bedside clock.

"Let's go downstairs and I'll put on the tea."

The front door opened and slammed shut. Joey came into the kitchen and screamed when he saw Annie. "I knew you would come! I just knew it. I prayed so hard to God and told Him all I wanted for Christmas was for you to be here. My prayers have been answered."

Annie laughed out loud and grabbed her little brother. "Why don't you go to the car and bring in my luggage. There's also a couple of boxes and I think there might be something for you in one of those boxes. Bring them in and put them by the tree."

While he was doing that, Rose and Annie moved into the living room and lit up the Christmas tree. The fire was burning and it cast a warm glow around the room. Joey opened the boxes and gasped at the beautifully wrapped presents as he placed them one by one under the tree. It all seemed so normal.

After Joey had gone to bed, Annie faced her mother and wanted to know exactly what was going on in her life.

"You seem very unhappy, Mom, and Joey has changed. He doesn't talk like he used to, and there is a sense of loneliness about him."

"It has not been easy being on my own. The friends your father and I had have suddenly disappeared. You certainly find out who your real friends are when you divorce. All of those friends I have known for years and now they barely acknowledge me when they see me on the street. But my big worry is Joey. He has not settled well into the public school. He is still keeping his grades up but he misses his friends and his hockey at the private school. There is just so much I can do but it never seems to be enough."

Annie put the tea aside and went to the bar. She made two cocktails and handed one to her mother.

"Why don't you and Joey move to Toronto with me? There is nothing to keep you here. It would be a brand new start. Think about it before you say no."

Rose smiled at her young daughter. She was so full of life, of promise and hope.

"That would solve a lot of problems, Annie, but there just isn't enough money to move."

Annie sat closer to her mother.

"When Joey finishes this school year, come to Toronto. Sell everything in the house that you can over the next few months, pack what you want to bring and ship it to me. You have sole custody of Joey, so Dad can't stop you. In fact, I would keep this plan close to your heart until you are on your way to Toronto because Dad will try and stop you. This will be our secret."

CHAPTER 30

Over the next few months Annie worked as many shifts as she could and was laying out a plan for the arrival of her mother and brother. There was a lot of money in her safety deposit box but she also knew it was going to take a lot of money to set up a home.

Opening the daily paper, Annie turned to the "Houses for Rent" want ads. Going down the many listings, she saw the perfect ad.

"Furnished three-bedroom, two-bathroom house for rent. Rosedale District, six hundred dollars a month, one-year lease" and the telephone number. This is the perfect location, thought Annie, for she knew St. George's Boys School was in Rosedale. She called the number and made an appointment to see the house the following day.

She parked her beaten-up old Studebaker a block from the address. The old bag of bolts was all she could afford since her father wouldn't let her bring her car to Toronto. Walking up the maple-lined street, she paused when she came to the house. It took her breath away. The gardens were beautiful and bursting with colour. She knocked the brass lion's head handle on the door and waited. A striking woman in her mid-forties greeted her.

"Hello, Anne," she said. "I'm Loretta Harrison. Please come in."

She took Anne's coat and hung it in the hall closet.

"Aren't you a little young to be renting a house?" she asked.

"Oh, I'm looking for my mother. She has been living out of town but will be returning soon. Could you tell me when the house is available?"

"It will be available in eight weeks for two years. I advertised early because I have so much to do before we leave. My husband has accepted a teaching position at the University of Montreal. Come, I'll show you through."

Bright sunshine came through the French doors of the living room, which opened to a carpet of emerald green grass with hedges of bright spring flowers. A solid oak staircase led to the bedrooms and at the end of the hall was a large sitting room that Annie knew would have the perfect light for her mother to set up her easel.

Mrs. Harrison showed her through the house, the last room being the family room. A floor-to-ceiling fireplace stood majestically on the far wall and on the opposite wall hung a large portrait of the Harrison family. Annie stared at the picture in utter disbelief: a portrait of the perfect family, or so it appeared. Were her eyes deceiving her?

"Are you okay?" Mrs. Harrison asked. "You look as though you have just seen a ghost."

Annie turned away and followed Mrs. Harrison back into the living room. She went over the lease very carefully. The possession date would be the first of July. Annie signed the lease and gave Mrs. Harrison the first month's rent along with a security deposit. They shook hands and Annie left with a disbelieving heart. The house was perfect.

It was a warm day and she decided to walk to St. George's Boys School, which was only ten minutes away, for her appointment with the headmaster. She walked by the playing field where a soccer game was in progress. To the left of the field was the hockey rink building, which she knew would make Joey very happy.

The main building was covered in ivy and the entrance had manicured lawns with masses of spring flowers. The headmaster's secretary met her at the door and escorted her to a reception area. The wainscot walls were covered with pictures of previous headmasters. A large showcase was filled with trophies that the school had won in various sporting events with pictures of the winning teams.

The reception door opened and Headmaster Armstrong walked in. He came toward Annie with his hand extended and introduced himself. She saw the glint in his eye as he took her in from head to toe and she knew there would be no problem getting Joey admitted for the upcoming fall term. She handed him a transcript of Joey's most recent marks and as he scanned them he looked over his reading glasses perched on his nose and nodded his approval. A half hour later she walked to her car with an even lighter heart.

As she started up the car it took several tries before the engine would turn over. "That's the next thing on my list," she thought. The old green Studebaker, which she had purchased with her savings from the radio station, was on its last legs. It had served its purpose but now she needed a reliable car, so she headed for the car dealership on St. Claire Avenue. An hour later she drove off the lot in a two-year-old yellow Mustang convertible. She checked her watch and drove to the club.

CHAPTER 31

Jeff was standing at the front door when Annie pulled up to Valet. He opened her door and took her dance bag from the back seat.

"Glad you're here, Orchid. The Doctor is in the house and waiting for you."

She laughed. "You can tell him I'm worth waiting for."

She checked in with the House Mom and saw Paradise sitting on the other side of the Dressing Room putting on her makeup. She went over and sat down beside her. They said hello and hugged each other as they got ready for work.

Annie put on her curly platinum wig, short emerald green velvet strapless dress and matching stilettos.

She patted Paradise on the shoulder and wished her luck.

"I need luck but you don't need any luck tonight, Orchid, the Doctor is waiting for you," Paradise said as she smiled up at her friend.

He was waiting for her outside the Dressing Room door and beamed when he saw her.

"I'm glad you're here, Orchid. I have something to tell you," he said as he led her to a corner seat. They sat together and he took her hand.

"I have accepted a teaching position at the University of Montreal and will be gone for two years. I will try to fly down every month or so to see you but my schedule will be very hectic. Here is my business card and if you should ever need anything, I beg you to call. I hate to leave and I am really going to miss you but this is an opportunity for me to advance my career. I have a little gift for you that I hope will remind you of me whenever you wear it."

He reached inside his suit coat pocket and pulled out a slim black velvet box and an envelope and he handed both to her.

"It is a small token of how much I like spending time with you. Please consider having dinner with me before I leave and we can talk about the future. You don't seem to have any goals. You're an intelligent, beautiful young woman and you should be in school. I can help you with that and all your living expenses. This is no place for a girl like you. Please think about it?"

Annie took the gift, brushing her hand across the soft velvet, and opened the box.

A stunning emerald and diamond bracelet lay on a bed of black satin. Annie took a deep breath and said, "It's beautiful."

He laughingly said, "It goes well with what you are wearing tonight."

He took the bracelet from the box, locked it on her wrist, and took her hand.

She turned the bracelet around and it sparkled in the lights. A tear slid down her cheek and the Doctor reached up to brush it away.

"Don't cry, Orchid. I will always be there for you. I have to go now but I'll be back."

The tear was not for the Doctor. She was thinking of the money she would not be making with him gone.

Annie went to the Dressing Room and put the bracelet and envelope in her locker. Paradise walked toward her.

"Is everything okay, Orchid? You seem sad," she said.

"I'm just tired, so I'm going to call it a night."

Jeff came into the Dressing Room. "The Doctor told me he won't be back for awhile. There's a regular customer in the club who has had his eye on you for weeks. Are you interested in dancing for him? He used to be the top criminal lawyer in the city but is now a judge. He has lots of money. C'mon and meet him."

Annie hesitated but went with Jeff, thinking only of the money.

She was introduced to Judge Anderson, a pompous, short, overweight, middle-aged man. He held an unlit, long Cuban cigar between his fingers and leered at Annie.

"Well, aren't you a pretty one and you sure have great legs. Now get up on the stage and show off those gams, and take it all off." He handed her a hundred-dollar bill.

She smiled down at him and said, "Don't waste my time."

******

Annie pulled her dance bag from her locker and put the bracelet and envelope in her purse. She tipped the House Mom, said goodnight to everyone, and headed for her car. Locking the car doors, she snapped on the interior light and opened the envelope. There was five thousand dollars along with the Doctor's business card.

Dr. Robert Harrison

Toronto General Hospital

She turned the card over and on the back was a note with a private telephone number. "Call me if ever you need me."

Her eyes hadn't deceived her.

CHAPTER 32

Annie waited impatiently for her mother and younger brother to come through the airline gate. She strained her neck over the other people waiting to greet family and friends. She spotted them and smiled. As she got closer to her mother she noticed a big change. Gone were the smiling eyes, but they held a glimmer of hope, and she had lost more weight. At the same time, Rose was thinking the young woman walking toward her was no longer her little girl but a very confident, beautiful young lady. She reached out her arms and enfolded her daughter. Joey had found their luggage and a Sky Cap loaded it into the car. On the drive home Joey kept up a constant chatter about his worries. "Where will I go to school? Will it be easy to make friends? And what about hockey?"

Annie put on her signal light and drove up the circular drive to their new home.

The sun was brilliant as she opened the tall, solid oak door and led her mother and Joey inside. The house was filled with flowers, a bottle of wine was chilling in the refrigerator and the cupboards were stacked with food. Rose stood in the hallway, looked around and then stared at her daughter.

"How did you do all this, Annie, and how can we afford it? I have so little money."

"The house belongs to a friend of mine who is working out of town for the next two years. It isn't going to cost us very much."

She looked around for Joey but he had already gone through the place and found his bedroom. Rose and Annie heard him yell and they made their way upstairs.

They found him in his bedroom sitting on the bed holding a little brown and white cocker spaniel.

"Is she really mine, Annie? The bow around her neck says she's mine. I've always wanted a dog." He snuggled his face into the puppy's soft fur.

Annie laughed. "Yes, Joey, she's all yours. Every boy should have a dog. Now come over here. I have something to show you."

She went to the window and pulled back the curtains.

"The building across the playing field, the one with the cross on top, is your new school. Their number one sport is hockey and Mr. Armstrong, the headmaster, is looking forward to meeting you. You are going to like it there."

Again, Rose stared at her daughter and started, "Annie how can we—" but before she could finish, Annie told her again not to worry.

"It's all taken care of," she said. She took her mother by the hand and led her into the sitting room at the end of the hall.

Rose gasped as she walked toward the easel that Annie had set up. She opened a wooden case containing tubes of paint and various brushes of all sizes. Joey came into the room and stood next to Annie.

Rose looked at her two children and put her head in her hands and cried.

"It's a new start, Mom. I hope you will get back into the art that you so love. You had such a passion for it years ago. I know that passion is still in you and you are going to be a great success."

Arm in arm, they went down to the garden. When Rose was settled in a comfortable patio chair, Annie handed her a glass of wine and told Joey to think of a name for his new puppy while she went to the kitchen to prepare dinner.

A half hour later Annie carried a tray of Caesar salad, warm garlic rolls, grilled salmon and fresh fruit and placed it on the patio table. She poured her mother another glass of wine and one for herself. As they enjoyed the dinner, Rose brought Annie up on all the news from home while Joey played with the puppy that he had named Spirit.

Annie cleared the table and caught her mother yawning.

"It has been a long day for you, Mom, and you must be exhausted. Why don't you turn in for the night and we'll have coffee in the morning."

CHAPTER 33

Annie threw her dance bag into the trunk of her car and wondered if it would be possible to leave it in her locker. She didn't want her mother to come across it. As she was checking in with the House Mom, Paradise came in behind her. She said hello to her friend and asked if they were allowed to leave their gear overnight.

"No, we have to take our stuff with us when we leave. There aren't enough lockers for everyone," Paradise replied. They headed across the Dressing Room and the House Mom called Orchid back.

"I can give you a locker, Orchid, because you are good to me and treat me with respect but it will have to be our secret." Annie thanked her and handed her a fifty-dollar bill.

A half hour later she was ready to go to work as Jeff came into the Dressing Room looking for her.

"There's a guy here who wants to meet you. He owns an art gallery but I doubt he has the money the Doctor has." Annie followed him into the club and was introduced to Tony Matthews. She sat down beside him as the cocktail waitress placed a silver bucket holding a bottle of champagne and two glasses on the table. She popped the cork and poured the bubbly liquid. Annie noticed a sketch pad on the table, picked it up and glanced through the pages of dancers in various poses.

He explained to her that he wasn't there to have the girls dance for him but instead he paid them to pose for him and he was hoping that she would be his next subject.

Annie smiled. "Tell me about your art gallery," she asked as she crossed her legs and looked at this interesting man. For the next hour he talked about his gallery and she listened carefully. The clock was ticking and although she wanted to stay and talk with him, there was no money on the table and she had to get to work. She stood, shook his hand and said she hoped to see him again but she didn't answer his question.

Over the next several months he dropped into the club often and Annie always spent an hour with him learning as much about his business as possible. He never again mentioned the possibility of her posing for him.

"Do you ever show new artists in your gallery?" she asked one evening.

"If their work is good. Why do you ask?"

"I have a friend who paints and I think her work is very good. If you're interested I could bring her to meet you."

The thought of seeing Orchid outside the club appealed to him. He thought he might convince her to sit for him. It was arranged for them to meet the following Monday, the day he viewed new artists' work.

CHAPTER 34

Annie pulled her long blonde hair back in a ponytail, put on pressed blue jeans and a white blouse. She looked like the girl next door. She hoped Tony Matthews would not recognize her.

"Are you ready, Mom? We can drop Joey off at his hockey practice and head on down to the gallery," Annie said as she loaded the car with her mother's work.

There was reserved parking for the gallery and Annie parked at the closest stall to the front door. The paintings were very large murals and they held them tight as Annie opened the door and a tiny bell rang. Tony came to the front to greet Orchid and was disappointed to find a woman and a young girl waiting.

He inspected Rose's work and was intrigued with the paintings of her whimsical characters. She explained to him that she loved painting murals of nursery rhyme characters on children's bedroom walls. He nodded his approval and was beginning to like this new artist.

As they talked Annie wandered around the gallery and noticed most of the art displayed was of nude or semi-nude women and the models were dancers from the Chatelaine Club.

She heard Tony and her mother approaching and turned around and saw them shaking hands. An agreement had been formed for Tony to arrange a show of Rose's work.

He held the door open for them as they said their goodbyes and when he shook Annie's hand a look of recognition showed on his face. He couldn't place this young girl but he knew he had met her before.

CHAPTER 35

The morning of the art show everyone was nervous. Annie was especially excited for her mother but she also knew that Mark would be driving down from Montreal for the show. It seemed like months, sometimes years, since she had seen the love of her life. The few times they did manage to see each other, there was never enough time. They would only have two days before he left again to fly home for a family celebration but he would be returning in a week to pick up his car, only to leave again for school. He had one more year before graduating from law school. They planned their future over many telephone calls and letters.

It was a clear, bright day as they arrived at the gallery and Tony anxiously met them at the door. A table of canapés was set up with a champagne table nearby. Flowers filled the room and their scent was soothing. Rose complimented Tony on the display, saying, "Calla lilies and stargazers are my favorite flowers. How did you know?" She also noted the beautiful orchids and told him they were Annie's favorite flowers.

He explained that the flowers had been delivered anonymously, as well as the case of fine champagne. "Whoever sent them has great taste," he said laughing.

Mark spotted a painting that caught his eye. "Let me be the first to purchase one of your fine works of art," he said to Rose. "I am sure this is going to be a sold-out show." And he reached for Annie's hand.

The invited guests flowed through the gallery and were surprised at Rose's genre.

"This is very different from any show you have had before," one of the guests said to Tony as she placed a sold marker on the largest mural with a price tag of fifteen hundred dollars. "This will be wonderful in my granddaughter's room."

At the end of the show all of Rose's work had been sold and the disappointed patrons who didn't get one placed orders that would keep Rose busy for several months.

Tony invited them to Chez Victor's for a celebratory dinner. Glasses were raised in a toast to Rose and to future shows. Annie and Mark left early and as they said their goodbyes Tony caught Annie's eye and was more certain than ever that he had met her before, but where?

All too soon Annie was driving Mark to the airport. It was a tearful goodbye but with a promise of the future. "Soon, Annie, we will be together never to part. I will always love you."

CHAPTER 36

"I am filled with happiness," Rose declared over coffee and croissants the following morning. "Never in my wildest dreams did I ever believe that I would experience such joy again. Thank you, Annie, for making it all happen. Without you I would still be grieving the loss of Timothy and the divorce from your father. I will never get over losing your brother but now I can see a future for myself."

"You did it, Mom. You are very talented. I just put things in place for you. I have been thinking that the sitting room isn't going to be big enough for all the work you have ahead of you. Perhaps you should open your own gallery with a studio in back where you could paint. There is an ideal location for lease in Forest Hills and I contacted the real estate agent. The rent is minimal with a one-year lease. I have made an appointment for you to view it tomorrow afternoon and if you like it, then we'll take it."

"Maybe that's rushing things. It might be better to wait awhile and see if I get more orders and have some revenue coming in. Where will the money come from to set up a new gallery?"

"Dreams don't wait, Mom. You've had experience in running someone else's gallery, now it's time to run your own. You might want to enlist Tony's help and I'm sure he would jump at the chance. I think he is quite smitten with you.

Rose blushed.

At two o'clock the next afternoon they arrived at the vacant space and the minute Rose walked in she knew this was where she wanted to be. "It's perfect," she said. Tony came along and within minutes took charge, designing the layout and negotiating the lease and leasehold improvements with the agent. In the end the rent was lowered and a one-year lease was signed to take effect in thirty days. Tony invited them to dinner but Annie declined saying she had to study but perhaps her mother would like to go.

The house was quiet and Spirit came rushing toward her but was obviously disappointed that she wasn't Joey, who was spending the night with a school friend. She walked away with her tail between her legs and went to her wicker basket.

In the kitchen Annie made a cup of tea and sat alone enjoying the quietness that surrounded her. She thought how her life had changed since arriving in Toronto three years ago and although it had been tough she always believed the adage that "when things got tough the tough got going." She put her teacup in the sink and settled down to study.

She felt a chill come over her and she got up to light the fire when the telephone rang. Another chill passed over her.

"Annie, it's Rebecca Cohen. There has been a terrible accident. Mark was hit by a drunk driver and we don't know if he is going to make it. The doctors are doing all they can but they are not hopeful. Please come home."

Annie pulled out her luggage and was packing when her mother walked in. She gave her the bad news and said she was catching a flight that was leaving in two hours.

"I'll come with you," Rose said.

"That isn't necessary, Mom. I can go on my own."

"I insist. I'm coming." She went to hug her daughter but Annie went rigid, and Rose felt helpless in comforting her. She knew the time would come when Annie would break down and Rose would be there to pick up the pieces.

She packed her bag as well as one for Joey and they arrived at the airport as the passengers were loading. They travelled first class and during the entire trip Annie never spoke a word. She was lost in her own thoughts.

Mark's parents met them when they arrived at the hospital. They stood outside the door as Annie entered his hospital room alone. His private nurse was sitting nearby. She nodded to Annie and left the room.

She walked slowly to Mark's bedside. His head was bound in sterile bandages with bright red blood seeping through, his closed eyes circled in black. The only sound was the bleep of the heart monitor. She took his hand in hers and spoke his name. She felt a faint squeeze and he whispered her name.

The bleep of the monitor became a long steady hum and reality stared her in the face. She was numb and could feel nothing, not even the hot tears flowing down her face onto the starched white collar of her blouse. A small moan escaped from the knot in her throat and her heart ached in the breathing silence. The pain locked her heart.

Three hundred people attended the burial. It was a sea of black except for Annie. She wore a white linen sheath dress with a matching coat and shoes and carried a bouquet of orchids, which she placed on Mark's casket. She stood next to his parents and they seemed to gain strength from each other.

Annie's father attended and he came to her and expressed his sorrow. Annie thought back to the time when he forbade her to see Mark. She suppressed her anger as he put his arm around her shoulder.

She gave her father a long hard stare and was shocked to see how he had changed. He had lost a lot of weight and his dark curly hair was now streaked with white. She asked him how he had been. He didn't answer but told her how proud he was of her and that she would make a great lawyer. He also told her that if he could do anything to help, he was as close as the telephone.

"Too late," thought Annie. "I don't need anyone's help; I will do it on my own."

Annie, her mother and Joey returned home the following day.

CHAPTER 37

"Welcome back, Orchid. You've been missed," the House Mom said as Annie dropped her dance bag on the floor, checked in and slipped a twenty in her tip jar. She walked across the floor to Paradise, who had her back to Annie but saw her in the mirror.

"I've sure missed you, Orchid and I'm not the only one. The good Doctor has been in several times looking for you as well as Tony, the artist. In fact, Tony is here tonight so hurry and get dressed and let's make some money. That is the name of this game."

As they dressed Paradise caught her up on all the news. Who had been fired and rehired, who got into a fight. "Nothing has changed," she said. "But everything had," thought Annie.

News of Orchid's return spread quickly throughout the club and Jeff came in looking for her.

"I told Tony you were working tonight and he wants you to join him. Do you want to do that? I know he doesn't spend a lot of money but he seems like a nice guy. What do you say?"

Little did Jeff know the extent of Tony's niceness. She would always be grateful for the break he gave her mother when he showed her work.

"Okay, tell him I'll be there shortly."

Annie was worried that Tony had recognized her at the art show but she already had a plan in mind if he exposed her. It was simple. If he did say anything she would make sure he never saw her mother again. A selfish thought on her part, but her mother must never find out how she earned her money.

Tony stood as she approached his table, extended his hand, and said it was nice to see her. He asked how she had been but she quickly turned the conversation to him by asking how his gallery was doing.

"I had a very successful showing of a new artist last week," he began. "Her work is different than anything I have shown in the past. She paints whimsical characters and creates an amazing fantasy. The show sold out, which wasn't surprising, but I was surprised when she leased space to open her own gallery. She is quite amazing and I like her very much."

Annie looked away because she didn't want him to see the proud look on her face. She had to be cool but Tony caught the look. Orchid was Annie, Rose's daughter. He was stunned.

He remembered the night they had dinner after the art show when Annie left early. Rose told him about her daughter, who was studying for her law degree and also had studied dancing. She had a part-time job dancing with a theater group. He reached for his drink and his hand was shaking. Rose didn't know her daughter was a stripper.

Jeff came over and whispered in Annie's ear that the Doctor was in the house and anxious to see her. Would she be long?

She spent a few more minutes with Tony and excused herself, saying a regular customer was waiting for her.

When she left, Tony thought about Rose's art show and the mysterious delivery of a case of fine champagne and orchids. Orchids.

Annie's stage name. It all made sense to him now. His eyes followed her across the room as she met the Doctor and flashed her biggest smile.

"You look wonderful, Orchid. I am so happy to see you and I have so much to tell you," the Doctor gushed as he hugged her.

The cocktail waitress placed a bottle of chilled champagne on their table and poured two glasses. He picked up his glass and made a toast to the future.

"My position at the university is ending sooner than expected and I will be returning home in a few months. My wife and I have decided to divorce. Our lawyers have worked out the details and the only thing remaining is to sell our house. I will be free, Orchid, and we can spend more time together outside this club. This is no place for a girl like you. Let me take you away from all of this shoddiness. Let me buy you a little house. You can go to school, be whatever you want, even a lawyer."

Annie cleared her throat. "Shoddiness? I don't quite understand why you would say that. If it's so shoddy, why do you come here?"

The Doctor was visibly shaken at her reaction.

"Oh, don't misunderstand, Orchid. I simply meant that you are smart and beautiful and with a good education you can do anything you want with your life and I just want to help you."

She glanced over her shoulder, looking for Jeff.

"I don't need your help. I'm doing fine on my own." She stood and abruptly walked away.

"He thinks he's my knight in shining armor," Annie thought as she made her way back to the Dressing Room. "He wants to buy me a house. Well, in one sense he already has." Her mind was racing with plans to buy the house that she had grown to love.

CHAPTER 38

Rose was preparing lunch with Joey's help when the front doorbell rang. "I'll get it," he shouted. Spirit started barking and followed him to the door as Annie came down from upstairs. A strange man was standing on the top step and Spirit started sniffing at his feet.

"Hello," he said. "My name is John Hanley and I am an attorney with the law firm of Willetts and Davis. We represent Dr. and Mrs. Harrison, the owners of this property. May I come in and speak with you?" He handed Annie his business card.

Annie led him into the living room and sent Joey back to the kitchen.

Mr. Hanley opened his briefcase and spread out several papers on the coffee table. Annie glanced down and saw a contract terminating her lease.

"The Harrisons plan on selling the property as soon as possible," he began. "I am aware that you have several months left on your lease and, if you are willing, they are prepared to buy out the lease and take care of any expenses you may incur in moving."

Annie asked if he would like tea and before he could answer she made her way to the kitchen, where her mother waited to find out who this stranger was and what he wanted.

While preparing the tea Annie told her the news.

"Oh, I will hate to leave this beautiful house," she said as she placed the teacups on a tray. "What will we do, Annie?"

Annie smiled.

"Don't worry, Mom. We're not moving because I plan on buying this place."

She returned to Mr. Hanley and sat down across from him. He looked intently at Annie. The sun was streaming through the open window and the brightness made her eyes bluer.

As she poured the tea she asked, "What is the asking price of the property?"

The lawyer was definitely taken by surprise as he lifted his teacup and handed Annie the details of the sale. The asking price was one hundred and eighty thousand dollars. If the purchaser was interested in buying all the contents except for the artwork, the price was two hundred thousand dollars.

Annie never flinched as she crossed her legs and gave it some thought.

"I'm assuming they are open to offers."

"That is possible, but it is priced well below market value only because they are anxious to sell."

"Well, I would like to put in an offer."

His teacup rattled as he placed it in the saucer. This was the last thing he was expecting. He pulled a real estate contract from his briefcase and wrote up Annie's offer of a hundred and sixty thousand dollars with all furnishings to be included. Her terms were fifty percent cash with the balance subject to financing. He handed the contract to her for her signature. Before signing she carefully went over the contract and, being satisfied, she placed her signature on the dotted line. At the door they shook hands and he assured her he would get back to her within twenty-four hours. As he drove away he wondered about the young lady he had just encountered. Although it was possible her offer would be accepted, it was not probable.

Rose and Joey were waiting anxiously for her and over lunch she told them that she had put in an offer of one hundred and sixty thousand dollars and her offer was to include all the furnishings. They would know in a day or so if the offer had been accepted.

"I can't believe they would even consider that offer, let alone accept it," Rose said. "This house is worth so much more."

"Well, Mom, it is better to go in low and if there is a counter-offer, then you know the price is somewhere in the middle. You can always up your offer but you can't go down."

"Even if the offer is accepted, where in the world are we going to get the money?"

"We can do this together. With what you have made on the sale of your art over the past year, and my savings, the financing won't be a problem. We'll go to the bank and get a loan."

Mr. Hanley called with the news that their offer had been accepted and recommended they go to his banker, Mr. McCarthy, who he had been doing business with for many years. A meeting was set up for the following Monday at three o'clock. Annie and her mother arrived on time but the banker was behind schedule. Rose was getting very nervous but Annie seemed to take it all in stride. "We'll get the loan, Mom. If not from this bank, then from another," she kept reassuring her mother.

Fifteen minutes later Mr. McCarthy's secretary led them into his office. He introduced himself and offered them a seat, apologizing for keeping them waiting. He opened a file folder and informed them the bank was willing to lend them the money they needed to purchase the house. After going over the terms and conditions, he handed the loan documents over to them for their signatures.

"Just sign on the dotted line," he said smiling. After all the signatures were in place, they shook hands and he congratulated them on their new home.

"You got quite a deal on that house," he said. "Mr. Hanley is still baffled that the Harrisons accepted your offer. No doubt it had everything to do with your terms and willingness to close immediately. Good luck."

Annie and her mother left the bank arm in arm with a satisfied feeling. Annie felt secure knowing that they would not have to move again; Joey and her mother had a permanent, safe place to live and no one could take that from them.

As they walked to the car Annie thought about her final law exams, which were coming up soon. She had three months left to do a lot of cramming but she also knew she had to work as her savings were depleted with the purchase of the house.

Pulling out of the parking lot, Annie suggested they pick up Joey at home and go out for a celebratory dinner.

"I would like to do that, Annie, but I'm having dinner with Tony. We are planning another show at the gallery and there is a lot left to do before the opening."

"Have you been seeing a lot of him, Mom? You haven't said anything to me about him."

Annie put the turn signal on, waiting for the oncoming traffic to pass and drove up to their front door.

"You've been so busy with your studies and performing in the dance theater that we haven't had much time to talk and catch up. I don't even know the name of the dance theater where you work. It would be nice to attend a show. If you would just let me know the date of the next performance then we could get tickets and take Joey."

"We?" Annie asked.

"I meant Tony and I could take Joey."

Annie turned off the car engine and took her mother's hand as they walked to the house.

"Be careful, Mom. You were married to Dad for a long time and things have changed since you last dated."

"What about you, Annie? You're young and beautiful and it seems you spend all your time studying and working. There is more to life than that. Isn't there a young man in your life? You never talk about what's going on."

"You're right, Mom. I don't have time and I'm not interested. They're all the same. You give your heart and soul to them and they just leave you in the end. When Timothy died he took a part of my heart with him and then Dad left. When Mark died, there wasn't much left of my heart." She brushed a tear back and said she was going to put on some tea.

Just after they got in, the doorbell rang and Spirit started barking. Rose picked him up as she opened the door and discovered it was a delivery of flowers. She signed for the long, silver box tied with dark blue ribbons then reached behind her for the jar of loose change on the hall table to tip the deliveryman and closed the door. Spirit's barking brought Joey and Annie into the living room as Rose opened the box.

"Who sent those magnificent roses?" Joey asked.

They were from Tony, and Rose was blushing.

"Who's this Tony guy, Mom, and are you going on a date with him? Is he the guy who helped you get the gallery opened?"

"Yes, yes and yes," Rose answered smiling. Her eyes lit up as she read the card: "Looking forward to seeing you tonight. Tony."

"Well, have a good time tonight," Annie said. "I'm working so will be home late."

Heading off to the Chatelaine Club, Annie went over in her mind all that she had to do before graduating in a month. She knew her mother never suspected that she was working in an exotic dance club and she was confident she would never find out. She drove to the back door of the club but a delivery truck was blocking her spot, so she carefully backed out and parked in front.

CHAPTER 39

Rose and Tony dined at The Bouquet, a small, very intimate restaurant owned by a French couple from Paris. There were only twenty tables, all occupied with couples making it very clear this was a restaurant for couples only. The owner's wife, Patrice, was wearing a black and white outfit with her hair pulled tightly back in a bun. She smiled and presented them with heavy leather menus. She reminded Rose of the nuns back at the convent. The tables were aglow with candles and flowers and their glasses of Beaujolais glistened in the soft light. Rose thought this must be how it was in Paris and, as though reading her thoughts, Tony asked her if she had ever been to France.

"No. I have only dreamed of going. It must be wonderful to visit all the art museums and see the works of the Masters. Just to walk the streets is a dream in itself."

He lifted his glass and proposed a toast to Paris. "We will go there one day soon."

They laughed together as they clinked their glasses and Rose realized just how much she enjoyed being with Tony.

Over dinner he told her about the time he spent at a gentleman's club drawing the dancers. It started with him just sketching the girls but soon one by one they came to his studio for a sitting and that's how his collection of "The Dancing Girls" started. The paintings were greatly received by his clientele. He offered to pay the girls but they refused, saying that they were flattered that he wanted to paint them and, besides, they made a lot of money dancing in their own way.

Lynne K Pettinger

"I don't know anything about that business but I wonder what would possess a young girl to make her living that way."

Patrice came to their table and topped up their wine.

"For most it's just circumstances of life. But there are a lot of the girls who are students working their way through university mainly because their families couldn't afford to pay for their education. By dancing, they are capable of making a lot of money quickly and can work on their own schedules."

Rose brought her hand to her forehead and felt as if she had been hit with a bat. "Could it be?" she thought. "No, that's impossible."

Out loud she asked, "Where is this club?"

"Not far from here. Why Rose, would you like to go to the club? You would be like a fish out of water. I'll drive by on our way home," he said teasingly.

Ending the dinner with a cognac, Rose was ready to go. She desperately wanted to drive by the club. Annie told her that she was working tonight but maybe it was in a different club than Rose thought. She could see the massive, brightly lit sign of the Chatelaine Club from two blocks away.

"Would you like to go in for a night cap?" Tony asked.

Rose scanned the parking lot and her heart stopped when she saw Annie's yellow Mustang. A small groan escaped and her hand went to her throat. Her stomach flipped upside down and she hoped she wouldn't lose her dinner. Her heart sank. Annie was dancing in a strip club to pay for her education, moving her and Joey to Toronto, buying the house and taking care of Joey's education.

Tony pulled the car to the curb and put his arm around her. "Are you okay, Rose? You look as though you have just seen a ghost."

CHAPTER 40

Annie rushed into the kitchen holding an armful of books, looking for her car keys. "Have you seen them, Mom? I'm going to be late for class."

"Annie, I need to talk to you. It's very important."

"I don't have time right now; I'm already late. We can talk tonight when I get home." She spotted her keys on the counter and when she turned to leave her mother was blocking the doorway.

"No, Annie. We are going to talk now? Where were you last night?"

Joey brushed by his mother and came into the kitchen. "I also need to talk to you, Annie." He waved a university application in the air. "I've decided to apply at the University of Montreal for the Faculty of Medicine and I need you to go over the application and make sure I haven't missed anything. I sure hope I get in."

"If that is what you really want, you'll get accepted. Your marks are excellent and Mr. Armstrong will write a superb letter of recommendation. Now, I have to run and I'll see you both tonight." Before Rose could say another word her daughter was gone. Annie didn't give another thought to the morning conversation. She was much too focused on getting to school, but it was different for Rose.

She spent the day wandering through their beautiful home with everything in place and sat in the garden overlooking the manicured lawn and banks of flowers. Annie organized all that by hiring Molly to keep the house in order and Jake to tend the garden. It seemed she had been organizing their lives for several years, daring anyone to say no to her. She had been right in most of her decisions especially in convincing her to move to Toronto with Joey. She had missed home but after awhile had given up hope that John would come after her and want her back. She thought about the letter she had received from Kate telling her that their father was very ill with a terminal disease and the prognosis was not good but he was getting excellent care and they were hoping for the best. He was able to work part-time at the law firm but had sold his horses, which broke his heart. She had told Annie about her father's health but there was no comment.

Rose had flashbacks to the Acres Stables and the tack room and at the same time said a silent prayer that his health would improve.

CHAPTER 41

Rose was sitting at the breakfast table when Annie came into the kitchen in a hurry as usual. She said good morning to her mother and poured a cup of tea.

"Anne Catherine, sit down. I want to talk to you," Rose said with a touch of anger in her voice. "You have been avoiding me for the past week and I will not tolerate it anymore. I want you to tell me exactly what has been going on in your life."

"I don't have time, Mom. Can this wait until I get home tonight?"

She worked late last night at the club and was going to be late for class but she also knew by the tone of her mother's voice that she had better take the time. When both her names were used, that was a clear indication her mother was very serious.

"No, this can't wait."

Annie carried her morning tea to the table and sat across from her mother.

"What would you like to know?" she asked defensively. She didn't believe her mother had any right to question her but out of respect she would indulge her.

Rose went straight to the heart of the matter.

"I want to know what you were doing at the Chatelaine Gentlemen's Club last week. You can't deny you were there because Tony drove by the club and I saw your car."

Annie shifted in her chair and wanted to make up some story but her intuition told her that her mother already knew.

"I was working, mother, as I have been doing for the past several years, even before you and Joey arrived."

Rose suspected her daughter had been stripping but to hear the truth was like being kicked in the chest. Tears quickly came to her eyes.

"How could you, Annie? How could you? I thought I taught you better."

"It's simple, Mother. I dance for the money. When I arrived in Toronto and Dad had refused to pay for my education, I was strapped for cash. There were days when I didn't have a lot to eat. I saw an ad in the paper for dancers and went for an audition. I had no idea it was a strip club and I wasn't going to stay but there was a girl there who had been dancing for a long time and she told me how much money could be made. I knew if I took the job I would never have to worry about money. There would be enough to pay for school and I wouldn't be hungry. It was a conscious decision and I have no regrets and make no apologies."

She left the table to get more tea and was surprised at how calm she was feeling. It was done; her mother had been told truth. She sat down, relaxed, and continued.

"I thought at the time I would work at the club just until I had enough money but it was so hard to walk away when I saw my bank account building up. The money was the motivating factor but I also learned that life is all about money. If you have it, it gives you power to do the things you want."

Rose was shattered to hear her daughter talk this way. "There's more to life than money, Annie."

Annie lifted her eyebrows and smiled at her mother. "Really, Mother? I'm not going to get into a philosophical conversation about money. I just ask, where would we be without it?"

Rose pleaded with her daughter. "You don't have to go there anymore. We have enough money. You will be graduating in a few weeks and will work at a reputable law firm. There is no need for you to continue. You can't go back there."

Annie reached over and hugged her mother.

"Don't worry, Mom, everything is going to be alright."

She looked at the kitchen clock on the wall.

"I have to go. I've already missed my first class. I know I've disappointed you but I haven't disappointed myself. Don't think about it; it will be over soon."

She kissed her on the cheek and left.

But Rose thought of nothing else throughout the day.

It was a miserable day with rain pouring down but it matched her mood as she paced the floor and thought about the morning conversation she had with her daughter. Annie's question of "Where would we be without it?" kept going through her mind like a sad song that wouldn't stop.

It was the money Annie made from stripping that brought her and Joey to this wonderful home; the money that gave Joey an expensive education; and she wouldn't have her art gallery without Annie; but did any of that justify Annie taking her clothes off for money and dancing for strangers?

All day she questioned herself as a mother. If she had known the money came from stripping, would she have moved to Toronto? Could she have stopped her? There was nothing she could do now, and Annie did say it would soon be over.

The rain had stopped and the sun came out. There was a beautiful rainbow after the downpour, which she saw through tears that were still flowing.

CHAPTER 42

The chancellor of the university announced her name and Annie walked across the stage of McGregor Hall and accepted her law degree as he shook her hand and congratulated her. She turned to her family sitting close to the stage and gave them a big smile. Her mother and sister Kate, who had flown in for the occasion, beamed with pride as Joey gave her the victory sign.

After the ceremony they met at the entrance of Convocation Hall and went to dinner at a nearby restaurant. Rose had invited Tony, with Annie's permission, and he was waiting for them and held a large bouquet of flowers with a perfect orchid in the center. The maître d' showed them to their table and poured the first glass of champagne that Tony had ordered. Annie noticed it was the same brand of champagne that she had sent to the opening of her mother's art gallery and she felt this was no coincidence, but she let that feeling go. This was her day and no one was going to rain on it.

Tony made a toast to the graduate, wishing her the best in the future then sat down across from her and asked what her plans were.

She reached for her champagne and smiled at him.

"I will be starting at Cooper and Tucker law firm next week and will be studying for the bar exam."

This afforded another toast.

They were all getting a little tipsy and it was time to leave. Tony excused himself, saying he had an early morning and no doubt Rose and her daughters had a lot of catching up to do.

When Annie entered the house there was another bouquet of flowers on the entrance table with a card. Rose and Kate knew the flowers were from her father and watched as Annie opened the card. The phone was ringing and Annie slipped the card into her pocket and reached for the receiver.

"Hello, Annie," he said quietly and that was all he had to say. She barely recognized his voice but she knew it was her father. He was the last person she had expected to hear from today. She realized upon hearing his voice how much she had missed him and how much time had passed. She cried like the little girl she had been. Rose, Kate and Joey disappeared into the kitchen and left her alone to talk to her father.

"Don't cry, Annie. This is a very happy occasion and I am so proud of you and what you have accomplished and you did it all on your own."

His breathing was becoming labored and he coughed but he continued despite his stress.

"It has been a long time since we have seen each other and there have been many changes in our lives. I know how much you were hurt when your mother and I divorced but that was between your mother and me, it had nothing to do with you. Your mother has forgiven me and has a full happy life in Toronto. Can you ever forgive me?"

Annie tried to pull herself together. There was so much that she wanted to say but the words just wouldn't come.

Her father's voice was fading and he started to cough violently and then the line went dead.

Kate took the phone from her and placed it back in the cradle. She put her arms around her sister and said, "Come with me, I have something for you."

They went into the living room and Kate handed her a note from her father.

Rose asked if they would like tea or more champagne. Annie voted for the champagne and she read the note. "This is for you, Annie. I love you, Dad" and enclosed was a check for thirty-five thousand dollars.

Annie took a deep breath and thought, "With this check, Joey's university education will be paid for and my dancing days are over."

CHAPTER 43

Her heels clicked across the marble foyer as she made her way to the bank of gleaming, brass elevators in the Cooper & Tucker Building. A group of five young men and two women were also waiting for the elevator car to arrive. Two of the men looked her way and gave her a big smile but Annie didn't respond as she glanced up at the floor indicator needle. The elevator arrived and the men stepped in, followed by the women. "Typical," thought Annie. "No chivalry here."

She stood with her back to the men and could feel their eyes on her and the questions they were asking themselves. The elevator arrived at the fifth floor and the men all moved at once brushing up against the women. The last man to exit brushed his hand across Annie's backside and in an instant she grabbed his wrist and gave it a sharp twist. He turned with a surprised look on his face but made no apology. One thing Annie had learned at the club was how to fend off roaming hands.

As the door closed the two women were smiling.

"That was a pretty fast move you made. I'm Marilyn and this is Beverly. You must be new."

"Yes, this is my first day. I'm Anne O'Brien."

"We work in the steno pool and if we can help you with anything just let us know. Where will you be working?"

"I'm here to article for the next ten months."

"Oh, you're a lawyer. Well, we won't be seeing a lot of you; the lawyers don't associate with us. We're just the drones."

The elevator arrived at the seventh floor and the girls got off. Annie held the door and said, "I'll see you."

Three more floors up and Annie was introducing herself to the receptionist. There was only a black telephone on her desk with four lights flashing. She picked up the phone, pressed a button and announced Annie's arrival to a voice on the other end.

Fifteen minutes later, Mr. Cooper greeted Annie and welcomed her to the firm. He walked in front of her through the main office to a meeting room where she was introduced to a junior partner. After a brief orientation she was taken to the area where she would spend the next ten months.

******

"Are you working again tonight?" Rose asked her daughter. "It seems we never see you and we miss you."

"Yes, it's work again tonight. These seventy-hour work weeks are getting me down but it won't be much longer. Two more months and I write the bar exams. I'm well prepared and know I'll pass. The firm has offered to pay for the exam and they have also indicated that there would be a position for me if I want to stay on with them."

Annie thought of how unfriendly a place it was. There was no time for idle chatter or socializing. Several of the lawyers had asked her out but her stony refusal soon sent them running. They had nicknamed her "Ice." She laughed to herself when she heard that. "Ice" was a dancer at the club. Her thoughts wandered back to the club, as they so often did. She missed Paradise and the camaraderie of the other girls and decided to go there Saturday night.

CHAPTER 44

She rang the back Dressing Room door and was buzzed in by the House Mom. She heard her hollering across the room, "Guess who's here? It's Orchid."

When she entered the Dressing Room she was met and hugged by ten girls and the questions came flying at her. "Where have you been? We were worried about you. Are you back to dance or just visiting?"

Annie heard Paradise's voice and smiled. "Give the girl some space, you're suffocating her." The girls stepped back and Paradise gave her friend a strong hug. "It's good to see, girl. I think about you all the time and keep waiting for you to come through that door, and here you are. Are you working tonight or just visiting?"

"I'm here to work and it's really good to be back."

"Well, let's get ready. There's a big bachelor party going on with lots of lawyers with lots of money."

She sat side by side with Paradise putting on makeup and getting dressed and felt at home. There was no pretence here, no one looking over your shoulder waiting and hoping for you to make a mistake. It was a safe feeling.

"Orchid, I heard you were here. Where did you park? I didn't see you coming in," Jeff shouted as he picked her up and hugged her.

"You have certainly been missed. particularly by a certain Doctor who comes in on a regular basis looking for you, but he is not here tonight. He'll be disappointed when he finds out you were here. He gave me his phone number to pass on to you. I know it's against the rules but he insisted and gave me a big tip."

From his wallet he took a tattered piece of paper with the phone number.

"Let's go, Orchid. The men are waiting," Paradise said. They left the Dressing Room together and as they passed the trash can Annie tossed in the ragged piece of paper.

The club was packed and noisy as Paradise led Orchid over to the bachelor party. Annie worked the group with her eyes and was shocked to find the elite from Cooper & Tucker smoking cigars, downing straight Crown and in general making absolute fools of themselves.

One of them grabbed Annie by the arm as she passed by him. She realized it was Mr. Cooper who was demanding a dance. He took a twenty-dollar bill from his wallet as she started to move away. He pulled her down on his lap and said, "You can't walk away from me. I'm a powerful lawyer and you're nothing but a stripper."

Jeff grabbed the obnoxious man as Paradise pulled her to her feet. Annie knew at that moment she would not be accepting the offer to join the firm of Cooper & Tucker.

She also knew this would be her last night dancing at the club. She pushed the Dressing Room door open and stood there for a moment thinking of the many nights she sat at the makeup mirror getting ready to entertain the customers. An empty box was on the floor and she picked it up and went to her locker. Costumes, stilettos and makeup filled the box and to her amazement she started to cry.

Paradise put her arm around her.

"Keep these things, Paradise. Perhaps someday another young and innocent girl will walk through that door and will need what's in this box. I won't be coming back."

Her friend held her closer. "Many say they won't be back but they always come back. You will be the exception. It's time for you to go, Orchid, time to hang up the stilettos and get on with your legal career."

"How did you know?"

"I just had a feeling. I will miss you, my friend."

CHAPTER 45

Annie grabbed her keys and hurried out into the dark morning. She wanted to beat the morning rush hour traffic and get to the office before another chaotic day began. She had a tough case to litigate in court and needed to go over every detail once again. She had learned a long time ago winning or losing depended on knowing the details.

Unlocking the door to her corner office on the thirty-fifth floor of the Bentall, Davidson Law Firm, the shrill sound of her phone ringing startled her. "This can't be good news," she thought. With a shaking hand she answered the phone.

"Anne O'Brien speaking."

"Annie, I'm so glad you answered," Kate cried. "Dad died an hour ago."

Seconds that seemed like hours passed.

"Annie, are you there, please say something. Tell me you will come home. I need you."

Kate, always the peacekeeper in the family who danced around the invisible elephant ever present in their home, needed her.

"I'll be there tomorrow morning."

She called her brother and asked him to go to their mother and break the news to her and to make arrangements for an early morning flight home and a rental car. She left for court.

******

It was a rough turbulent flight and the three of them held hands to get through it. Anne reminded her mother and Joey that they had been through many rough times during the past years and they would get through this because they had each other.

She put her head back on the seat, closed her eyes and took a deep breath and let her mind go back over the years. She wondered where she ever got the fight within her to carry on despite the times she didn't think she would make it. The thought of failure made her shudder. She couldn't fail, she wouldn't. She wanted to prove to her father that he wasn't needed, that she would make it on her own, and she had done just that. And now did any of that matter?

She was startled out of her reverie by the pilot's voice announcing that they would be landing shortly. She looked over at her mother and realized she was crying.

"Are you okay, Mom? We'll get through this, too."

They unfastened their seat belts and stood in the aisle with the other passengers, waiting while the ground crew moved the stairs to the airplane door. They hurried down the stairs in the pouring rain and made their way across the tarmac to the terminal. Joey waited for their luggage and Anne went to the rental counter to pick up the keys to the car that Joey had reserved.

CHAPTER 46

The rain was falling in sheets and the banging of the windshield wipers was mesmerizing when Anne pulled up to the solid brick house. The front porch light was on and Kate stood in the doorway waiting for her family. The two sisters hugged and entered the house together, one sobbing, the other with a hard look on her face as she worked the room with her eyes.

Sitting on the couch against the bay window was Father O'Reilly, an unwanted portion of the past. He stood and extended his hand to her.

"Welcome home, Annie. Despite the unfortunate circumstances, it is good to see you." Anne said nothing, as she was more interested in knowing who else was in the room. It was an awkward moment for the priest and, as if reading her thoughts, he said, "The others are waiting at the funeral home. A High Mass is planned for seven o'clock." He looked at his watch and suggested they leave.

Mr. Fitzpatrick greeted them and offered his condolences. On a table nearby was a recent photograph of her father next to a silver tray holding prayer cards. Low music was coming from another room and the scent of the overflowing flowers was stifling. Grief, like the rain, was everywhere.

Anne slipped through the mass of black clothes and made her way to the chapel alone. She could hear the murmur of voices as she stood at the chapel door. Terry was reciting the rosary with a group of people when she looked up and saw Anne. The praying stopped immediately and Anne could feel the years of resentment and hatred toward this woman well up in her. She walked toward Anne and the others discreetly left.

It had been decades since Anne had laid eyes on this woman whom she blamed for breaking up her parents' marriage, the woman who stole everything from her. For years she rehearsed in her mind all the things she would say to her if ever given the chance. This was her chance but she walked past her and took the few remaining steps to the open casket.

She started to feel faint and reached for the prayer bench to steady herself. Kneeling, she reached in and touched her father's hands, which were entwined in a crystal rosary that she had given him one Christmas when she was a child. She remembered holding his hand when she was a little girl.

She touched his face, which had a serene, peaceful look as though he was ready to meet his Maker, and with that touch all the love she had for her father came tumbling back as her tears fell on the white satin lining of his casket.

She felt an unfamiliar touch on her shoulder. She didn't turn around but in that moment she felt a deep sadness for this woman who had loved her father. The woman who took care of him for years and tended to him when he was dying was now alone with a broken heart. She reached up and took Terry's hand. No words were needed and Anne felt the misplaced hatred for this woman leave her.

For the first time in years she felt free.

Dance In My Shoes

PART 2

THE SEVEN INCH STILETTO FLEW
OVER ANNE`S HEAD
THE SHOES WERE OFF
THE FIGHT WAS ON

CHAPTER 47

Anne Baxter boarded the early morning flight hoping to catch up on the paperwork that was slowly taking over her life. Settling into first class, she glanced to her right and noticed the seat next to her was unoccupied.

"Let's hope it remains that way," she muttered to herself.

Just before takeoff a young girl boarded the plane escorted by a Sheriff. Anne found herself annoyed but curious about the young girl's situation and the Sheriff's attitude. The girl seemed like a reluctant passenger and looked frightened. She was dressed in blue jeans with the knees ripped out and frayed at the hem. A white T-shirt bearing the slogan "What Happens in Vegas, Stays in Vegas, Baby" was falling off her thin shoulder. She wore a pair of expensive designer sandals on her feet, feet that needed a good wash and pedicure. Her ash-blonde hair kept falling over her eyes and she continually flipped it back. She was trying very hard to stifle her sobs with head bowed, pulling at an overused balled up tissue in her hand until it was a shredded mess on her lap, which she brushed onto the floor of the aircraft.

Anne reached into her tote bag for a travel pack of tissues and a bottle of chilled water, which she offered to the young girl. As the girl lifted her head in thanks, Anne looked into very sad blue eyes with tears clinging to long dark lashes. In a small voice she thanked Anne.

"Where are you going?" the girl asked.

"To Albuquerque," was Anne's reply.

"Oh, I'm going home to St. Louis, but I'll be back."

"Prepare for takeoff," the pilot announced.

A pretty flight attendant with a name tag that read "Jennifer" stood at the front of the cabin giving instructions on what to do in an emergency. Her message blasted through the overhead speakers, but no one was paying much attention.

Once airborne the captain turned off the seat belt sign and the flight attendant rolled the breakfast cart down the aisle. Before Anne could put cream in her coffee the young girl had devoured her food. Silently, Anne slid her untouched tray toward her. After she finished the last crumb she told Anne her name was Melissa. She was seventeen years old, about to be eighteen in a few months. She came to Las Vegas after graduating from high school. Her parents were dead set against it but, with money given to her for a graduation present, she bought a one-way bus ticket to Las Vegas to get a great job and she just knew one was waiting for her.

Anne took the young girl's hand and listened as the sobs began and the story tumbled out.

"Las Vegas was booming. There were thousands of jobs," she exclaimed. But she soon found out you needed more than a high school diploma to get a really good job. She was hired as a cashier at a deli for six dollars an hour. Her meals were free and she had a room in a boarding house, not in a very good area but it was cheap. She was lonely and thought about going back home but didn't want to hear everyone saying, "I told you so, I told you so." It was hard to make friends in this city. She couldn't go into the casinos or any clubs because she was too young. And then she met Mike.

"He came into the deli one day," she said. "He was real friend-ly and good-looking. He knew his way around Vegas and drove a big fancy black Lexus with tinted windows. Had a real nice apart-ment that was gated with a real person in the gatehouse. No one could ever get in there if they didn't belong. The guard even carried a gun."

She didn't know what Mike's job was but he was always busy at night. He told her she was pretty enough to be a dancer and could make a lot of money, as much as ten thousand dollars a month. All she had to do was talk real nice to the customers, do a dance or two for them and they would give her money. It was easy, fast money.

Melissa sat back in her seat and let out a sigh.

"Would you like a soda or anything more to eat?" Anne asked becoming quite intrigued with Melissa's story.

"A soda would be real nice."

Anne asked Jennifer, the flight attendant, for a cold soda. Jennifer looked down at Melissa, rolled her eyes and went to get the drink.

Holding the soda and wiping down the condensation on the can, Melissa explained to Anne that you needed a Sheriff's Card to dance and, more important, you had to be twenty-one to dance. Mike said he would take care of that; she was not to worry. He knew people. He got her a fake ID and Sheriff's Card. She left the boarding house, moved in with Mike and began taking her clothes off for a living at a local strip club. There were two other girls living at Mike's place. They were also dancers and Mike told them to teach her how to use the pole. There was a floor-to-ceiling pole in his living room.

"Imagine that," Melissa said. "A brass pole in the middle of the living room. Mike thought of everything."

She had been dancing just over three months and things were good until two days ago when Vice busted the club. They arrested her for having fake ID and took her to jail. Now they had kicked her out of the city, but she would be back. Mike would be waiting for her. She tried to phone him but he didn't answer his cell phone. "Probably forgot to charge it," she said. Mike was holding her money for safe-keeping. There were a lot of thieves in Las Vegas, he had told her. Her money would be safe with him. He would meet her outside the club when she finished work and she would give him the money she made. On most nights she would make eight hundred dollars, on a good night a thousand. Mike would always give her a couple of hundred dollars she could spend on herself. She lifted her left foot in the air and said that she had paid four hundred dollars for her sandals, but they were Jimmy Choo's. She figured Mike had about twenty-five thousand dollars of her money. It only took her three months to make that much. Why, that was almost as much as her father made in a year. Yep, she was coming back.

"Prepare for landing," the pilot announced.

Anne gathered up her belongings, said goodbye to Melissa and wished her well.

As she picked up her rental car and headed to her business meeting, Anne couldn't shake Melissa from her thoughts. "What would become of that young girl?" she wondered. Chances were she would never find out.

CHAPTER 48

Another flight, another meeting. Anne had had her fill of airports and stuffy meetings with overbearing lawyers who felt she was the token female on the Board of Directors of their very prestigious law firm. This would be her last trip. She was resigning and looked forward to taking some time off — well-deserved time off — to be spent catching up with family and friends. She wondered what tomorrow would bring and what new challenges awaited her.

During her first week of being unemployed, she met Danny and Beth, a young couple who bought the house next door to her. They more than fit the image of the All-American couple and an instant friendship developed. Sitting outside enjoying the summer evenings, watching the desert sunsets and sharing a bottle of wine, she got to know them very well, or so she thought.

Beth, a tall blonde, twenty-three-year-old flawless beauty modeled three evenings a week and was studying Science at the university. Danny, a handsome, six-foot-two, twenty-six-year-old who had proudly served his country in the Marines, he declared to Anne, was working on his MBA and tended bar at a casino restaurant the same evenings that Beth worked.

On a sunny Thursday afternoon, Beth came home early from school. She knocked on Anne's door and fell into her arms. Her whole body was shaking and she complained that her head was pounding; she had the chills and every part of her hurt. Anne put her to bed in the guest room and made a pot of chicken soup while Beth slept. When she woke several hours later she sat up in bed and Anne handed her a cup of soup. She sipped at the soothing broth.

With both hands wrapped around the soup cup, holding it close to her mouth, she looked across at Anne and said, "You would make a great House Mom, Anne. You are so thoughtful and you really care about people."

"What are you talking about?" Anne asked with a little laugh.

"I told you I modeled at night and I did for awhile but I wasn't getting enough work, it is so competitive in this city. Danny and I needed money so I applied and got a job as an exotic dancer and I've been dancing for two and a half years."

Beth read the blank look on Anne's face.

"I'm a stripper, Anne, a stripper. I didn't want to tell you because I didn't want you to think I was a slut or a bad person."

"Beth, what a person does for a living doesn't define the kind of person they are."

"Danny and I aren't happy about this but it is the fastest way to make the money we need. We don't have any bills or student loads. We have managed to save fifty thousand dollars for our future and, as you know, our house is ours, no mortgage."

Anne had often wondered how this young couple could afford such a high-end house with a designer pool, a white BMW for Beth and a red Corvette for Danny. Now she knew.

"My parents don't approve but they don't have the money to pay for my education and I sure don't want to claw my way through university ending with a stack of bills and student loans. When we graduate, we plan to get married.

"Most strip clubs have House Moms. They take care of the girls and make sure they are perfectly groomed before starting work. They bring them food but mostly they just listen and give a hug when needed. I wish there was an opening at the club where I work. If you would be interested, call Larry at the Tiger Club. He's one of the managers there. He knows everything that goes on in the clubs around town. If they don't have an opening maybe he knows of a club that does."

Danny knocked on the door, looking for Beth. He picked her up as if she was as light as a feather, thanked Anne for taking care of his precious lady and took her home with the remaining soup.

As she prepared for bed, Anne wondered what she could possibly offer a Las Vegas strip club. That world was in her past, far removed from her present life.

She had attended the best Ivy League university and graduated cum laude, but it wasn't easy with classes in the day and working three nights a week to make ends meet. She could certainly empathize with Beth. It was even harder after her parents divorced. She insisted that her mother and younger brother move to the city where she was studying and together they would make it. It was a long hard climb but they did it. She had fulfilled her goal after graduating to be accepted into the best law firm, where she climbed the corporate ladder — but at a price.

It cost her marriage. With the heavy workload and travelling that her job demanded she didn't have too much time to think about Philip, her estranged husband, but every now and then he would invade her thoughts and the memories would come flooding back. How she adored him! The funny way he had of brushing back his hair when it fell over his eyes, crystal blue eyes that seemed to dance whenever he looked at her, and the way he made her laugh.

They met when the United States law firm where he was a partner merged with her Canadian firm. She remembered the strong handshake he had when they were introduced and how every nerve in her body tingled with that simple touch. They left that meeting together and went to her favorite restaurant, The Bouquet, a little French bistro on Broadway. They talked for hours until they noticed the staff had left and the owner was waiting patiently for them to leave. They were married six months later at that same French bistro with Anne's entire family in attendance. "It's about time," her younger brother, Joseph, exclaimed. "After all, she is thirty-five years old." Her sister Kate was there along with her husband, Tom, and their twin daughters, and Anne's mother, Rose, gave her away. Soon after, they moved to Las Vegas when Philip became senior partner in the law firm.

"What went wrong?" Anne thought. "Why didn't I see it coming?"

It wasn't that they fell out of love, just that they seemed to grow apart, giving priority to their careers. There was never enough time. They separated after ten years of marriage, five years ago. Funny, they never divorced, just went their separate ways. And now that she had kicked that oh so important career aside, she had time on her hands, but no Philip.

"Enough with the lamenting," she said to herself. "Maybe I do need a drastic change in careers. I'll make that call tomorrow. Nothing ventured, nothing gained."

She turned out the lights and slept.

CHAPTER 49

The following evening after several attempts, Anne finally reached Larry at the Tiger Club. The loud background music prevented any semblance of a conversation but the few words that Anne was able to catch were, "Okay, come and see me tomorrow night at eight o'clock."

Prepared for the interview, Anne left her home dressed in a conservative navy blue business suit, with coordinated leather pumps and bag and resume in hand. She found her way to the club and as she parked her car she was stunned at the number of very expensive vehicles in the overflowing parking lot. The oversized sixty-foot-high neon sign, "The Tiger Club" with flashing five-foot-high bright red lips, beckoned the patrons.

Stepping out of her car she locked the doors and walked toward the gleaming, massive red and gold entrance. Halfway across the parking lot she was stopped by an enormous man who looked down at her and asked, "What can I do for you?"

"My name is Anne Baxter and I have an appointment at eight o'clock with Larry."

"Are you sure you're not a narc or from probation?" he laughed.

With no reply from Anne, he told her his name was Jeremy. He was the head doorman and would radio Larry and let him know she was there.

Jeremy was six foot seven, three hundred pounds, with arms as thick as the trunk of an old oak tree, whose manner could be very intimidating to some people. He was wearing a tuxedo shirt with a red bow tie that seemed to be choking him. The rolled-up sleeves revealed tattoos of tigers. "A real company man," thought Anne.

As she waited for Jeremy to make contact with Larry, more foreign cars pulled into Valet, and men stepped out of their cars handing bills to the attendant and slapping each other on the back.

"Have a good night," someone shouted.

"I will if Sophia is here," another answered.

As the massive doors opened to let the men in, the music flowed out.

"Okay, Anne, let's go," Jeremy said as he took her by the arm and escorted her into the club. She entered darkness, heard the music, saw the colored lights but couldn't get a secure footing.

"Takes a second or two for your eyes to adjust, it's very dark in here. C'mon, sit at the bar, order a drink and I'll go get Larry."

Opposite the bar was the stage, surrounded by men in their expensive suits with the lights catching the glitter of their diamond pinkie rings. Champagne buckets sat on their tables. Men wearing baseball hats stood at the bar holding cold beers. Regardless of what they were wearing or drinking, all eyes were on centre stage.

A tall blonde dancer with a chiseled, tanned body, who seemed as comfortable in her seven-inch stiletto heels as she would be in a pair of bedroom slippers, stepped up onto the stage. She gracefully climbed the polished brass pole until she was out of sight. Wrapping her long legs around the pole with her body parallel to the stage below, she slowly, with great strength and poise, moved down the pole to the rhythm of the music. Before reaching the stage she pulled her body up, grabbed the pole and swung her body around until the clear see-through stilettos softly touched the stage. The crowd roared and applauded. A bouncer was nearby to help her pick up the bills — of all denominations — that were being thrown by the dozens onto the stage. As the dancer left the stage, Anne caught her breath and smiled to herself. A burly voice interrupted her thoughts.

"You must be Anne. I'm Larry. Hey, Rocky, bring us a drink. What'll you have, Anne? Have you ever danced?" Larry asked, all in one breath, as a tall, well-dressed man approached.

"Hi Jim, this is Anne, here for the House Mom's job," he chuckled.

Anne stood and as they shook hands Jim told her he was the general manager. "Come to my office where it's quiet and we can talk."

He led her to a wood-paneled door and punched in a code. The door opened, revealing a room lined with surveillance cameras, several desks and a bank of computers. An Italian black leather sectional sat in one corner.

"Sit down here, Anne," Jim said as he pointed to a casual leather chair in front of his desk. He perched himself on the corner of the desk and looked down at her, asking, "Where do you come from? What's your story? You are so out of place in a joint like this. Have you ever been a stripper?" He laughed out loud to himself. "Can't imagine you ever stripping for a living or, for that matter, can't imagine you as a House Mom. You're sure not typical. This is a rough business. Most of these girls are all screwed up, there are fights, they steal from each other and the competition is fierce."

"Not so different from the corporate world," Anne thought.

"Most of the guys who come in here are the pillars of society," Jim continued. "Judges, doctors, senators, lawyers, movie stars and super sports jocks, you name it and they're here.

"We have Vice in here one night getting their rocks off and the next they're back trying to shut us down, and here I am looking at you, wondering what the hell brought you here. You're class, but you know this place can use some class. Be here tomorrow night same time for training. Stella's the House Mom tomorrow night. She's been here a long time. House Moms don't usually quit around here because they make a lot of money. But it just so happens that one of the House Moms is leaving the state; husband got transferred, so her position is open. Stella is good; she'll teach you everything you need to know."

He picked up his radio and summoned Jeremy, who, within seconds, was at the office door to escort Anne to her car. During the forty-five minutes Anne was in the club she spoke less than a dozen words but she did grasp that this world was ruled by men, the women to be seen and not heard, again not so different from the corporate world.

During the drive home she giggled to herself thinking what her family and friends would think of her working in a strip club. She could well imagine her sister Kate's reaction. "Have you lost your mind?" she could hear her saying. "Mom will faint and Dad will roll over in his grave." Her younger brother, Joseph, would probably ask if he could get in free. She giggled some more.

CHAPTER 50

The following evening Anne arrived promptly at eight o'clock.

"You're back," Jeremy greeted her. "Jim isn't here yet but I'm to take you to the Dressing Room. Stella knows you're coming."

He was holding a long, thin silver flashlight. "Grab onto this, I don't want to lose you in the crowd." She took hold and followed his six-foot-seven frame toward the Dressing Room, not missing the two pairs of handcuffs hanging from his belt or the mini stainless steel baseball bat.

He guided her through the club, arriving at a filthy purple door plastered with vulgar stickers and stubs of chewing gum with a tattered sign reading "The Dressing Room." As he pushed open the door, Anne looked into a massive room full of activity. Hair dryers whirred, hot curling irons stood on stands, and loud chatter filled the room, with girls coming and going in all manner of dress — some in fluffy slippers wearing bulky bathroom robes, sweats, jeans and oversized T-shirts. A makeup artist in one corner worked on a dark-eyed beauty; in another corner a gray-haired woman sold costumes hanging from racks; a masseuse worked out the aches and pains of a dancer, who complained about her knees and feet.

"How long do you think these knees are going to hold?" she said to no one in particular. "And my feet, my poor aching feet. These old dogs have been dancing in these fuckin' heels for nine years." She picked up her seven-inch stilettos that were perched on the back of the chair next to her and dropped them. "I'm going to be thirty years old in a couple of weeks. Damn, I hope this body holds out for another six years and then I'll retire."

"No you won't," said a dancer leaning up against the lockers smoking a foreign cigarette. "The money is too good. You know it and so do I. Maggie is still dancing and she's forty-five years old, been dancing for twenty-four of those years. Her three kids are attending some fancy university in Palo Alto, so she ain't goin' anywhere and neither are you."

Jeremy introduced Anne to Stella. "Sit over here, Anne," she said. "I'm just checking in these girls."

Sitting on a high stool, Anne worked the room with her eyes, taking in as much of the chaos as she could. It was non-stop. She glanced over at Stella: overweight, rough, wearing jeans and sandals, with a cigarette hanging from her mouth, long acrylic nails painted bright red. When she finished checking in the girls she lit another cigarette and tossed the pack to Anne.

"This place is such a dump. These girls are just slobs; I would hate to see what their homes are like. They throw everything on the floor, never clean up their messes, no respect," she said with disgust.

Anne noticed the overflowing ashtray on the desk. Trash was thrown on the floor and half-empty cocktail glasses with soggy cigarette butts were scattered over the counters.

"Jim told me you never did this job before, so let's get started on what a House Mom does," she continued as she stubbed out the half-smoked cigarette. "The girls pay to work here. It is called a tip-out or rent or house fee. Everybody calls it something different; here it's a tip-out. You collect the sixty-five-dollar tip-out from each girl and put it in the cash drawer." She slid the drawer open, slammed it shut and locked it. "Always keep it locked."

Stella continued, "The girls come to the back door and ring the bell. You can see them in the monitor. There are lots of cameras outside. Buzz them in. When they are inside the outside door locks and they come up to the Dressing Room door and you buzz them in, but before you do, check the monitor and make sure no one has followed them in. It's kinda like they're in a holding cell. If any drunken customer decides to follow them in — and it has happened — call Security and they will take care of the drunk. The girls have to show you their Sheriff's Card, can't work without one. Make sure they haven't expired. You'll get cards that seem a little different and you can bet they're phony but it's tough to tell, they sure do a good job of forging. Just a few months ago, Vice made a bust here. Caught one of our girls with a forged Sheriff's Card and not only that, she was under-aged. They put her on a plane back to her home state. A shame really, she was a good dancer, never made any trouble but her pimp kept her in line. Mike is his name. He is well known in the business. She was so young, never believed for a second he was a pimp. So much to learn."

Melissa danced into Anne's thoughts.

"They also need a Business License and that sets them back a hundred bucks but the Department of Taxation needs their piece of the pie. How many girls actually file taxes is anyone's guess, not too many is my guess, and they must fill out a Metro Police Card. There is no glass allowed in the Dressing Room. Not because glass might get broken and a girl might step on it but because those glasses make good weapons when hurled across the Dressing Room aimed at a dancer's head. They can't chew gum. The owner hates gum. He came in here one night wearing his Gucci loafers, stepped in a wad and shit hit the fan. Definitely, no gum. They have to work a minimum of six hours but you'll get girls who'll be here an hour or two and want to leave. A sure sign they are leaving with a customer. They'll give you some excuse, like they forgot their extra shoes or costumes or whatever at home and they will be right back. True to their word they are back in a couple of hours but ten to one their leaving had nothing to do with missing shoes."

A dancer with a dollar bill in her hand asked Stella for a cigarette. She took the dollar and handed the girl a cigarette and at the same time lit one for herself.

"Most of the girls are pretty good," Stella went on, "but there are always a few rotten apples in every barrel. One girl had her RV parked in the back parking lot and was servicing the guys between dances until management found out.

"The House Moms bring food for the girls. Anything you want." Anne looked across the wide, dirty desk covered with bits of dried cheese, potato chips and a few crackers.

"The girls tip you for the food. Bring a tip jar, that's how we make our money. Oh, yeah, we get a check from the club that doesn't amount to a hill of beans. Bring anything and everything you might have in a medicine cabinet: tampons, Polysporin, toothpaste, mouth-wash, hair spray, cotton balls. They forget this stuff, which is good for us because they tip plenty. Also, bring cigarettes. They will tip you a buck for one. Don't get involved with the fights, call Security on your radio and let them handle it. If the girls are caught fighting, they are fired and they sure don't want that. Every dancer wants to work here. It's the busiest club in town and they make a ton of money but sometimes tempers flare and the fight is on. Don't put up with any of their crap."

Stella buzzed a dancer in the back door and reached for her ciga-rettes, not realizing she had one burning in the ashtray.

"Jim said you are going to start on the morning shift. The morning girls don't meet the criteria for the afternoon shift or, God forbid, the night shift. The night shift dancers are all a bunch of prima donnas. They can work any shift. You might get a few on the morning shift depending on their personal schedules but not many. I probably won't see you again because our shifts don't cross. Good luck, you're gonna need it."

CHAPTER 51

Over the next few days Anne and Beth shopped for a few outfits that would be appropriate for her new position as House Mom: flat shoes, dress pants, several tops and sweaters. A far cry from her power suits. Beth filled Anne in on what the girls at her club liked their House Moms to bring. "Lots of salads, healthy stuff. They will love you for it and they will be generous with their tipping. You're going to be great. I'll be thinking of you tomorrow when you start your first shift."

They said their goodbyes and hugged, with Anne promising to call Beth to let her know how her first day went. As Anne entered her home the phone was ringing. She reached for it as she laid down her parcels.

"Hello," she answered. It was Bob, the morning manager, calling about her shift.

"You won't have too many girls, twenty max. Your shift starts at 3:00 and goes until 11:00 am. Be here fifteen minutes early and park at the rear of the building. Andy, the Valet guy and Joe from Security will be watching out for you. They'll help you in with your stuff. See ya' tomorrow." The phone went dead.

Anne loaded up her car at 2:00 am the following morning, a little nervous but excited about starting on a new path. She knew if she left by 2:15 she would have plenty of time to reach the club and be on time. It seemed odd to be going to work at this time of the day. Heading down Tropicana Avenue she was amazed at the bumper-to-bumper traffic and wondered where all the cars were going. At 2:45 she pulled up to the back door of the club and as promised Andy and Joe were waiting to help her in with her things. When everything had been unloaded Anne thanked them and said, "If you boys would like to come back when I have everything set up and have a bite to eat, by all means come. I should only be about thirty minutes or so."

Anne brought out a basket of cleaning supplies and scrubbed down the filthy desk and chair she would be using. The security camera she was to "keep her eye on" was thick with nicotine and it took twenty minutes to get it clean.

She spread out a white linen tablecloth and arranged platters of fresh fruit, home-baked muffins, bagels and a variety of cheeses and juice. When she turned around, a beautiful blonde stood before her.

"Who are you and what's with this fuckin' spread? Who's it for?" the blonde demanded to know.

"I'm Anne and I'm your new House Mom. What is your name?"

"I'm Tara, one of the night girls, and I'm trying to decide if I'm going to stay for the morning shift or not," she said with attitude.

"Well, Tara, this spread is for you," Anne began, "and before we go any further, let's get one thing straight. You will not use that language around me. Is that understood?"

"La-de-dah," Tara said. "Hey, everyone get a load of this. We have a new House Mom who doesn't like my potty mouth." But there was little reaction to what Tara had to say because something else was going on in the Dressing Room.

Across the room, voices were raised and chairs were being pushed aside. The girls had formed a circle around two fighting dancers and were encouraging one or the other to make the first blow. Their voices got louder and bets were being taken as to who would win the fight.

A seven-inch stiletto heel flew over Anne's head. The shoes were off. The fight was on.

Anne made her way over to the circle of dancers and stepped into that territory. "What's the problem?" she asked.

"This raggedy trick was trying to make time with my man and I'm gonna snap her fuckin' neck," a tall redhead said as she lunged for the other girl.

Anne took another step closer. Her heart was racing so fast it felt as if it was going to burst out of her chest. She hated violence but she knew she had to remain calm if she was to maintain control of the Dressing Room.

"Not on my shift, you're not," she said with a firm voice. "You're here to work, not to fight. You're here to make money, not trouble. Now, please get back to work, but before you do, clean up the mess that you have made on the floor."

Everyone looked down at the floor where a dozen or so acrylic nails were scattered, a blonde wig, large glittery hoop earring and three stiletto heels, the fourth being the one that narrowly missed Anne on the other side of the room.

"Clean it up?" they shouted. "What do you mean clean it up? That's your job."

"Just what I said," Anne answered sternly. "Clean it up." She turned, her heart still pounding, not realizing that she was being followed by a dozen girls who ignored the mess on the floor.

"Why didn't you call Security?" they asked.

"You know the rules. If you get caught fighting you will be fired and I'm guessing that you need your job. And while you are all gathered here I have a few rules of my own. There will be no cussing or swearing. You will treat me with respect and I will respect you. Is that clear?"

They all nodded.

"Are we allowed to eat this food?" someone asked.

"Of course, I brought it for you, but not until your mess has been cleaned up."

As a team they scurried over and picked up their things as well as the other trash on the floor. Then the hungry girls gathered around the food. "Wow, this is great We never get stuff like this. Where's you're fuckin' tip jar, Mom?"

Anne looked up and was about to say something when Tara interrupted. "You're not to swear. Apologize, you moron, or I'll knock you off your shoes. And her name isn't Mom, it's Anne. Her tip jar is right there in front of you. Now drop in a twenty and you can have some of her food."

The offending dancer apologized and, with an almost wishful look in her eyes, said, "Yeah, you're right, Tara. Anne would never have a daughter like me but if I had a mother like Anne I wouldn't be a stripper. 'Fuck' was my mother's favorite word. Oh, sorry, sorry."

"My mother's idea of a hot meal was throwing a Hot Pocket in the microwave," said another dancer. Everyone laughed.

Anne put her arm around the offending dancer. "You can call me Mom. And what do I call you?"

"My name is Shelly. I'm a night girl and I've been working here a long time."

The other girls overhearing wanted to call Anne "Mom" also. So, her new identity was simply Mom. She liked the sound of it.

"Have you always been a House Mom?" one of the girls asked. "Where did you work before you came here? You're really different from the other House Moms. They don't really care about us, they just want to be tipped. What did you do?"

"I worked in a law office," Anne answered.

"What? Are you a lawyer? You can't be serious. How much money did you make as a lawyer, maybe a hundred and twenty thousand, maybe a hundred and fifty? Last year I made two hundred and seventy-five thousand dollars, all cash, tax free," the young dancer declared, rocking back and forth on her stilettos with a silly grin on her face. "And I just went to grade ten."

"Big deal," came a voice from across the room. "Crystal made more than that."

Before an argument started, Anne admonished, "Well, you won't be making that this year if you don't get back to work." They all laughed.

As they were walking away, Anne heard one of the girls say, "We're not going to get away with very much, not with this House Mom. She seems to have the answers before we have the questions."

CHAPTER 52

After several months the girls on Anne's morning shift had increased in number. She now had seventy girls. There had been no fights or stealing, but occasionally swear words would fly and voices would be raised. But one look from Anne and the matter would be settled. The girls called it "the Mom look."

They were taking better care with their makeup, nails and hair, asking Anne for advice on what outfit looked best, did the color suit them and should they wear their hair up or down, wig or no wig. Several asked for advice regarding money.

"What do you do with money?" twenty-two-year-old Dana asked one morning. At five feet four inches tall, weighing a mere one hundred and ten pounds. Dana, in her stilettos, would ask Anne if she wanted a lap dance. "Only twenty dollars, Mom," she would say and they would both laugh. "I've been dancing a little over two years and have saved a bit of money," Dana said. "Don't know what to do with it. Have it hidden in my condo but I worry someone will find it and then it's gone."

"It depends on how much money you have, Dana," Anne said. "If you want to invest your money, then real estate is a good avenue."

"I have eighty thousand cash. I should have triple that for the time I have worked but you know what they say: easy come, easy go."

Anne introduced Dana to Rebecca, an honest, knowledgeable real estate agent who had sold Anne her house. Two months later Dana reported back that she had bought two houses, one for her and the other a revenue property that she had rented out. "I'm on my way to becoming a tycoon and when I hit my thirtieth birthday I will retire and just collect rents," she said. "If I could only get on the night shift, I'd make it by my twenty-fifth birthday but the managers here are so pigheaded they don't even know we exist. All the shift managers are so possessive of their girls. If we even mention we would like to be upgraded they throw a fit because that is money out of their pockets. That's all they care about. They don't give a rat's ass about us, and besides, I wouldn't get to see you. It wouldn't be the same coming to work and not finding you here."

"Point taken, Dana, but there is more to owning property than just collecting the rent. Have you thought of taking a property management course? There is a good one offered at the community college."

"Oh, heavens, I couldn't go to college, Mom. I didn't even finish high school. You have to be smart to go to college. I'm just a stripper, and besides, I have to work. No one takes care of me but me."

"You don't need a high school diploma to take certain courses at the college," Anne advised. "Anyone can attend and It doesn't cost a lot of money. This can be done on your nights off and, while we are on this subject, it would make a lot of sense for you to get your General Education Degree. It's something to think about. Remember, the water doesn't flow until the tap is turned on."

"Thanks, Mom, I'll think about it."

Anne packed up her supplies and was getting ready to end her shift when the house phone rang. It was Jim, the general manager, and he wanted to see her in the office. She asked Shelly to watch the monitor as she picked up the keys to the cash drawer and walked toward the filthy purple door, making a mental note to talk to Marco, the night porter, about getting it cleaned. Dan, the morning bouncer, pushed the door open and said he was to escort her to the office.

When she stepped into the club the girls saw her and started hollering and whistling. "Hey, there's Mom. What are you doing in the club, Mom?" The customers looked at Anne with curiosity as the dancers explained to them who she was and what she did.

Jim was watching the office camera as Anne and Dan made their way through the club. He opened the door, pointed to a chair and told her to take a seat.

"It seems your reputation as a good House Mom has spread among the girls," he said. "The morning girls are looking great and they seem to have a different attitude. What a change. The bouncers are ticked off because they're never summoned to the Dressing Room to break up a fight. You know, they get a kick out of watching the girls tear into each other; it breaks the monotony. My problem is a lot of our best night girls are now working the morning shift because of you. We need those girls at night so I've decided to put you on the night shift, but remember, the night girls are a different breed from the morning crowd, major egos, prima donnas, up-and-coming movie stars, or so they think. Can you handle it?"

Before Anne could reply, he said, "Good, take the next couple of days off. Your shift will be Wednesday through Saturday starting at 7:00 pm and ends at 3:00 am. You will have about two hundred girls to put up with. The night manager is Frankie and he usually arrives around nine o'clock. You won't see him for awhile; let's just say he's spending some time at Club Fed."

He turned, picked up the phone and Anne knew that was her dismissal. But she waited. Jim put down the phone and asked, "Is there something on your mind? Do you have a problem with this change? You know, you're lucky to be getting this shift. I have more than a half-dozen House Moms who would give their eye teeth for the night shift. Stella sure as hell isn't going to like this change." He picked up the phone again.

"Well, there are several morning girls who, I believe, met the criteria to work the night shift. Would you consider upgrading these girls?" Anne could see the look of shock on his face. He dropped the phone.

"What? Who do you think you are coming in here and talking about upgrading girls? You're just a fuckin' House Mom. I'm the only one who has the power to upgrade any stripper. You have a lot of nerve," he said as he hammered his right fist into his left palm.

Anne lowered her head slightly and then looked up at him. "I was just thinking of you, Jim. I can only imagine how tough a job you have running the club. Why, with more than two hundred girls on the floor along with eight hundred customers you have a thousand potential problems. I don't know how you do it."

He leaned back in his black leather chair and looked at her, tapping a pencil against his lower teeth.

"What girls are you talking about?" he asked.

Anne stood up and opened the door. "I'll give you a list."

Dan was waiting for her. "What was that all about? Man, it doesn't pay to upset the boss. I heard him hollering and thought for sure you were going to get canned. Don't mess with him."

Anne just smiled as he walked her back to the Dressing Room. She had met many men like Jim over the years and it was just a matter of knowing how to handle them.

The girls were waiting for her. They handed her five one-hundred-dollar bills. "Our customers wanted to know who you were, so we told them everything you did for us and that we love you. They wanted to thank you for taking such good care of us." Anne then told them she would no longer be working the morning shift but had been moved to the night shift.

"Oh, no! What are we going to do? It won't be the same without you."

CHAPTER 53

As Anne started her first night shift she looked up into a very familiar face. The dancer handed over her Sheriff's Card and said her name was Sonya. She paid her tip-out, smiled at Anne and got on with her business. After an hour or so, she was ready for work and, on her way into the club, she stopped at Anne's desk.

"Thanks for your discretion," she said. "I don't know who was more surprised tonight, me seeing you here or you seeing me. I'm still a little shaken up. How do I explain my being here?"

"You don't have to explain anything to me," Anne said.

"Mrs. Baxter —" she started. Anne interrupted her and said, "Please call me Anne."

"Anne, I make more money dancing three nights a week than I do in a month as your bank manager. No one at the bank knows I dance and I would lose my job if they found out. The funny thing is most of the guys at the bank are in here at least a couple of nights a week, throwing money around, playing the big shot. They also have their childish little contests as to who can steal part of a dancer's outfit. They have no idea how much these outfits cost. At work they have a box in their locker room filled with stuff they have stolen from dancers. They call it their trophy box. They're the guys who struck out at the nightclub before coming here and it is their twisted little way of getting back at all the women who rejected them. They are pathetic creatures."

Sonya continued, "They brag about their little conquests at the office and it's all just a total exaggeration. So many times I have wanted to give them a piece of my mind but I know it wouldn't do any good. Fortunately, I have never been recognized. When I put on my costume, the wig and all the paraphernalia that goes with it, I barely recognize myself, and I always work the opposite side of the room from my fellow bankers. I'd quit the bank and dance full-time but I stay because banking is a credible profession and it offers a good benefit plan with medical. I'm a single parent with two kids and dancing supplements my income."

Anne was listening with much interest.

"There are many single moms working here," Sonya went on. "It's ideal for them. They put their kids to bed and the nanny is there to watch over them, as well as a nanny cam. You see the girls pulling their laptops out of their lockers checking in on their kids. They come to work, put in their six hours or so and go home. When the kids wake up in the morning, Mom is there and will be all day. How much better can it get?"

Sonya started to turn toward the door. "I must get to work," she said, "but I was waiting for my closest friend, Jennifer, to arrive. She's a flight attendant for a major airline. You're really gonna love her. She hasn't worked for awhile. Vice busted the club not so long ago and they arrested a young stripper for having false ID. They put her on a plane and sent her home. Jennifer worked that flight. A passenger wrote a letter to the vice-president of the airline and lodged a complaint that Jennifer needed an attitude adjustment. She was suspended for a couple of months all because of a scruffy little kid and a nosey passenger who didn't know the kid was a stripper. I can hardly wait for you to meet her."

Melissa again invaded Anne's thoughts along with Jennifer's condescending attitude. It was comforting to know that it had been adjusted.

"When Jennifer arrives, will you tell her I'm in the club and can we keep my dancing just between us?" Sonya asked.

"Of course," Anne said. "Mum's the word."

CHAPTER 54

It was close to nine o'clock and Marco, the night porter, entered the Dressing Room on schedule to empty the trash. He always came in quietly, would nod his head in greeting to Anne and get on with his work. They had never exchanged many words but tonight Anne wanted to talk to him. She took a twenty-dollar bill from her purse and tucked it into the palm of her hand. He was a shy fellow who didn't have a great command of English but he would certainly understand a twenty-dollar bill.

"Hello, Marco," Anne said holding the twenty-dollar bill discreetly but so Marco could see it. She asked him if there was any chance he had time to scrub down the filthy purple door and scrape off the vulgar stickers and wads of chewing gum.

"Oh, sure," he said smiling. "After work I come back and do whatever you want."

"Good, and perhaps tomorrow night you might have time to wash down the lockers. They really need a good cleaning." He returned after his shift and the transformation of the Dressing Room began. He scrubbed the purple door almost down to bare wood. In the supply room he found an old can of purple paint and gave the door a fresh coat. The following night he tackled the lockers. Within a week the makeup mirrors were gleaming, ashtrays emptied and washed, counters scrubbed down. He found an old vacuum cleaner in the back room and cleaned up the carpets.

Anne was very grateful and gave him a generous tip. She also noticed that the girls tipped him, commenting on how the Dressing Room even smelled cleaner.

"Let's work together and keep it this way, nice and tidy," Anne said.

CHAPTER 55

There was a line-up of girls checking in earlier than usual. A big convention was in town and they were getting ready for a bumper night. A man in his mid-fifties walked into the Dressing Room. In a split second the energy changed and an icy chill crept in, dispelling the general chatter and laughter. He stood no more than five foot six, wearing a tight black silk muscle shirt. Showing through the shirt was a solid six-pack that one could use to scrub clothes. Several thick gold chains and a large crucifix hung from his neck. His shoulder-length blue-black hair was so thickly sprayed it probably wouldn't move in a gust of wind. His little brown eyes, set close together, were on the girls. Anne studied him and came to the conclusion that he was definitely a product of the small man syndrome.

The girls cheered and greeted him, "Hey Frankie, how's it going? Where have you been?" Several girls shouted out and came up to give him a hug as his short stubby hands roamed over their bodies. A few minutes of that and he told them to get back to work.

He swaggered up to Anne's desk. Stepping behind it, he took her in from head to toe. "So, you're Anne, the new House Mom. I'm Frankie, your manager. Couldn't be here when you started; had other business to attend to. Jim told me you were a looker and had some brains, rare in a woman. Just want you to know if any of these bitches give you any trouble you're to call Security and they'll handle it. Understood?"

"That part I understand but what I don't understand is why you call the girls bitches? Can you explain that to me?" she said icily.

"Ha! Jim was right again. He said you were feisty. What did you do before you came to work here, break balls? That's none of my business and I really don't give a damn, just curious."

"You didn't answer my question," Anne said.

"Well, as time goes on you'll learn. You'll learn that these girls are disposable. They come; they go. One walks out and a hundred want in. This is the number one club in town. Don't you get it? Everyone wants to work here. There's never a shortage of girls at The Tiger Club, hell, they're nothing, easily replaced," he said with a dirty laugh.

"Nothing?" thought Anne. "Just your mortgage payment and car note, keeping you in a high standard of living. They have the power. They don't know it yet, but they will."

"Maybe some night we can have a drink and I'll teach you the ropes of this business," Frankie said. "What do you say to that?"

"The chances of that happening are slim to none, Frankie," Anne said laughing.

"Ha! We'll see, we'll see," he said as he turned on his two-inch heeled cowboy boots and left the room, waving as he went. When he left, the girls came over to Anne and told her how much they hated Frankie.

"Well, I would never have guessed that by the way you were hugging him and telling him how great he is," she said.

"Oh, we have to, Mom, otherwise he would make our lives miserable on the floor and mess up our money. You don't know what it's like out on the floor," said Shelly.

"Dealing with the bouncers and DJ shaking us down for more than the ten percent we have to tip them is one thing but you don't want to be on Frankie's bad side. If a customer so much as touches our leg, Frankie is all over us like a wet T-shirt if we've pissed him off. Being on Frankie's bad side means a bad night. He demands so much from us."

Bridget leaned against Anne's desk. "Yeah, that's how it is unless you're Bangkok Jane," she said. "She can do anything she wants, a total exception to the rules. She should be working the lounges in the casinos because she is definitely a prostitute but she doesn't think so. So long as she has the protection of the bouncers, she's safe. She must tip Frankie and the bouncers a good five hundred a night but that's nothing when she's making thousands. It's bad for us. We can be doing a clean dance in the VIP room and next to us she's giving her customer a hand job or blow job. Our customer sees that and he wants the same thing. I would rather walk out of here with a thousand bucks than stoop so low as to do the nasty for an extra thousand or so."

Frankie called Anne on her radio. "Is Shelly in the Dressing Room? I thought I saw her there. Send her to the office." The radio went dead.

"God, how I hate that man," Shelly said. "I thought being locked up might have changed him but no, no such luck. You know what he wants, don't you, Mom? Use your imagination. He thinks I should be flattered because I'm the flavor of the night."

"Does this happen often?"

"Oh, yeah, every night, sometimes twice a night. He just picks who he wants and away we go."

"Well, doesn't that put you in the same class as Bangkok Jane?" Anne asked. "The only difference is she's getting paid for the dirty deed."

"Never thought about it that way but I guess you're right, but I also need my job."

"Have you ever thought of saying no?"

"Good God, no. You don't say no to Frankie."

"Why don't you try?" Anne suggested. "Just say no. Has anyone been fired because they said no?"

"I don't know anyone who has said no. We're all afraid of losing our jobs," Shelly said, smashing her cigarette out in the ashtray.

"Well, perhaps it's time someone did say no."

"Ah, Mom, you don't understand. Frankie has always crossed the line."

"And he will continue to do so until you draw one, a thick one," Anne said.

Frankie called Anne again on the radio demanding to know what was keeping Shelly. "Tell that broad to get in here now," he hollered.

Shelly stood up, adjusted her G-string and touched up her make-up. The click of her stilettos had the sound of thunder as she headed toward the purple door. She wasn't gone long. Less than five minutes later she rushed into the Dressing Room, flushed and shaking.

"I did it, Mom. I did it. I said no to Frankie. He flipped out. I told him I was drawing the line and I wasn't taking him around the world one more time. He just laughed and said there was a line-up of girls waiting to service him and he threw me out of the office."

Frankie was on the radio again demanding Ashley to the office. Shelly hurried over and told her to say no. "He won't fire you, Ashley. God, what a high saying no to that slimy cockroach. You can do it too, Ashley, we all can."

After the fifteenth call to Anne, Frankie gave up. The girls gathered, high-fiving, hugging each other, and danced around the Dressing Room. They were bound together by a special force. They had made a choice. They said no. The line had been drawn long and deep.

It seemed they were holding their heads higher with smiles on their faces as they went into the club.

Frankie didn't appear in the Dressing Room for a week.

CHAPTER 56

It was going to be another busy Friday night. The club was packed with a long line of men waiting to get in. Anne looked up from her desk and found Frankie standing there with his hands on his hips, tapping his foot against her desk.

"Do you know what the fuck is going on?" he burst out. "Every bitch in this place has ignored me for the past few weeks. Oh, yeah, they're polite enough, too polite. What the hell is wrong with them? They just work, rarely get drunk, they don't fight and they treat me like I'm the boss."

"You *are* the boss," Anne said.

"Yeah, I know but things are different. I need some new girls. Jim gave me a list of morning girls; he has a good eye for upgrading them. They're real hungry to get on the night shift and I'm auditioning four of them tomorrow night. There's a pretty young thing on the list. Dana is her name. Send her to the office as soon as she is dressed. I want to look her over, if you know what I mean. Make sure she's in something really sexy, the less the better. I hear she's more than anxious to work my shift."

The following evening, on time, the four girls arrived. They hugged Anne and said they couldn't believe they might get upgraded. Dana was the last to hug Anne. She clung a little bit longer and then stepped back and smiled. "Mom, I have so much to tell you and you have no idea how much I have missed you," she said.

"Well, we'll talk later but now you must get dressed. Have your hair and makeup done then come see me," Anne said.

They were like school girls, giggling and excited just to be considered. An hour later they were back and presented themselves to Anne. Dana stepped up dressed in a very flimsy outfit leaving little to the imagination. She looked ten years older.

"That's a very nice outfit, Dana, but do you have a wrap," Anne asked.

"Oh, yes, but I hear Frankie likes real skimpy."

"Well, let's get the wrap and see how it looks."

Dana returned with a beautiful black lace wrap, which Anne tied around her slim hips. "Yes, that is much better. Now before you see Frankie I want you to meet Shelly. She has worked the night shift for a long time and she can give you some good tips."

Shelly was watching from across the room and came over to Dana.

"Hello, Dana," she said. "I'm Shelly. Come over here with me for a minute." They walked off together, the seasoned dancer guiding the young one.

Anne inspected the other three girls and sent them to Shelly. Then, saying a silent prayer, she radioed Frankie that Dana was on her way to the office. It wasn't long before she returned.

"Oh my God, Mom, do you know what he wanted me to do. I said no just like Shelly told me. He said he would kick my ass back to the morning shift. Oh, lord, I really want to work nights and be back with you. I guess I blew it... no pun intended."

"It isn't over yet, Dana," Anne said.

The other three girls returned with the same story.

Frankie was blaring over the radio for Anne to come to the office. She chuckled to herself. The other girls burst out laughing. "It's your turn, Mom. You go, girl."

When Anne reached the office, Frankie was pacing the floor like a bear with a sore paw.

"What the hell did you tell those girls?" he demanded to know. "Has everyone gone crazy? What's wrong with those bitches? They never said no to me until you came here."

Anne was proud of her five-foot-nine height. Even with the two-inch shoe lifts Frankie wore, she was still taller. She looked down at him.

"If you continue to threaten the girls because they don't meet your demands, you are going to have a major sexual harassment charge brought against you. This charge will attract the media and believe me they will jump all over this. They love this kind of stuff. Is that what you want?"

"Sexual harassment? Get real. You don't have a clue what goes on in this club." He stopped and stared at her. "Are you trying to threaten me?"

"Absolutely not Frankie; no threat, it's a promise."

He looked up stunned and dropped his hands to his side, frustrated. "You think you're pretty smart, don't you? You may win this one but just remember I can have your job. Jim may think you're the best thing since sliced bread but I still have some power, don't forget that."

Anne returned to the Dressing Room to find that the morning girls had changed into their street clothes with their makeup and costume bags by their feet, waiting to say goodbye. They looked so disappointed.

"We really wanted to work this shift and be back with you," they said with tears in their eyes.

"Well, what are you doing out of costume?" Anne laughed. "You had better get back into your gear and get to work. There are many customers waiting to meet you."

Anne called Shelly over and thanked her for her help and asked her to keep an eye on the girls.

"I don't know what you said to Frankie to get those kids on your shift but it must have been something that staggered him. I would like to have been a fly on the wall when that conversation took place," she said with a grin.

Four hours later Dana returned to the Dressing Room. "Oh, it is so good to be on this shift, Mom. I can't believe how much money I have made in just a few hours and I have four more hours to work. I've already made a thousand dollars. She slipped a fifty-dollar-bill into Anne's tip jar. "Do you have a minute? There's so much I want to tell you."

Anne settled back in her chair.

"Since we were last together, which is about seven or eight months ago," Dana began, "I have bought six houses with the help of your friend. I also called the college and took the property management course and at the same time got my General Education Degree and now I am studying for my real estate license. But I don't want to just buy and rent houses, I want to design and build them. Next semester I'm enrolling at the university to study architecture.

"How has all this happened so quickly, Mom? I would have nothing but a lot of designer handbags, clothes and expensive lunches to show for my money if it hadn't been for you. Why did you care? Nobody has ever cared about me. My mother was a junkie who handed me over to Family Services when I was ten years old. I was passed from one foster home to another and suffered a lot of abuse. At fifteen I ran away from the last foster home because my foster father molested me. It was a terrible time for me, but I survived. I never dreamed I would ever get an education but look at me now! And it's all because of you."

"Dana, you did all the work. I just showed you the way. I am very proud of you. Just remember when you hit the tycoon level, always sign your own checks and pay your taxes."

CHAPTER 57

Anne was clearing off her desk getting ready to call it a night when Shelly came into the Dressing Room.

"Those new girls are doing okay, Mom. They have what it takes, which is quite surprising considering the night crowd is so different in that they have the big bucks and egos to match. Little Dana sure has the gift of gab but she is a smart cookie. She just danced for a lawyer who comes in on Friday nights looking for the new young dancers. He's pretty well known in the city because of the ads for his law firm with his face plastered all over billboards. He thinks he's God's gift to women but those who know him know that he's nothing but a pedophile."

Anne interrupted her. "A pedophile? That's a pretty harsh label to put on any man. How do you know he's a pedophile? Has he had any convictions?"

"No, nothing like that but we all figure he has to be because he always wants us to change into a little school girl outfit. You know the outfit. Short skirt with a white blouse, knee high socks, the Mary Jane patent leather shoes and always the hair in pigtails. He took a real shine to Dana but she was onto him before any damage was done. Too bad Shirley hadn't been as smart."

Shelly lit a cigarette while Anne answered the door and checked in three dancers.

"Shirley left the business before you came here but I remember the night Mr. Bigwig set his sights on her and charmed the G-string off her. She fell into his trap and not a tender one. She was so young, a couple of years out of high school, just a naive kid from a small town in Missouri. She was completely dazzled by Las Vegas and the crazy money she was making. Against all the rules and my talking to her, as well as a dozen other girls, she didn't listen and met up with him outside the club. He took her to dinner and gave her a thousand dollars for gambling. They were having a great time but before she knew it she found herself in a hotel room being raped and beaten to a pulp. God, it was so sad."

Shelly took a drag off her cigarette and continued. "She pressed charges, but of course the charges were dropped. After all, she was just a stripper. His story was she came onto him and tried to steal his money. To add insult to injury, this club, the great Tiger Club, a Gentlemen's Club — now there's a good laugh — fired her because the case attracted so much media attention. God, there were reporters hanging outside the club for nights on end. Management went nuts because business was off. Shirley went back to Missouri. These kids come to Vegas believing they are going to make it big but for most this city chews them up and doesn't spit out their bones. You have to have skin as tough as rawhide to make it in this business."

She put out her cigarette in the ashtray on Anne's desk and yawned. "Well, I'm going to call it a night," she said. "I'm tired, and for working as hard and as long as I have, I'm leaving with only twenty-eight hundred dollars after tipping out the bouncers and Frankie. Dana will be checking out too, she told me she is leaving when you do. Oh, here she comes now."

Dana came through the purple door carrying what looked like a bunch of hay that she tossed into the trash. It was obvious that she was very upset as she went up to Anne and Shelly. "What's wrong?" they asked.

"I can't believe that Frankie. He introduced me to a big shot politician from Hawaii and handed me this grass skirt and lei. He told me to put them on and dance for the guy because he has lots of money and is very important. He also told me this guy wanted to take me to Hawaii for a vacation."

"Yep, and if you go, Frankie will also get a free trip for him and his family," Shelly said.

"I'm not going anywhere with that creep. He is so fat and ugly and has really bad breath. I don't want to dance for him."

"Did he tell you his name, Dana?" Anne asked.

"Oh, yes, he even gave me his business card, bragging that he's a Senator," she handed the card to Anne.

"What am I to do, Mom? I don't want to get fired," she said with tears welling up in her eyes.

"Don't worry about it, Dana. Get changed and we'll leave together."

Anne picked up her radio and called Valet to bring Shelly and Dana's cars to the back door. Frankie heard Anne's call to Valet and was soon standing in front of her desk.

"Dana isn't leaving. She has a date with one of our special customers. Get into the grass skirt, Dana. What this guy wants, Frankie delivers. Hurry up, he's waiting," Frankie said as he stared at Anne, daring her to defy him.

"Dana isn't going anywhere but home."

"The hell she is. You think you're so fuckin' smart but you're not, you're nothing but a fuckin' House Mom and I can fire you anytime I want. You keep up this Miss Goody-Goody attitude and sure as hell I will fire you. You better watch your step."

"How dare you? Don't you talk to Mom like that," Dana said.

He turned and saw her opening the door to leave. "Get back in here," he growled as he reached for her and pulled her back.

Anne stepped between them.

"Now Frankie, this can go one of two ways. Dana can go back into the club and entertain your powerful Senator. It's possible, but not probable that she will leave with him. It is also possible and very probable that some reporter is lurking around outside wanting a good story. Or Dana leaves now as she has finished her shift and no doubt, you being as savvy as you are, can find a willing dancer to please your Senator."

She gave Frankie a very serious look and held up the Senator's business card. Frankie reached to snap it out of her hand but he wasn't fast enough. He slammed his fist on the desk and stomped out of the Dressing Room, banging the purple door hard against the wall.

Andy rang the bell announcing that the cars were outside. It was time to leave.

CHAPTER 58

Ninety vases of flowers filled the Dressing Room with an overwhelming fragrance. Roses, orchids, stargazer lilies, and more exotic flowers of the like Anne had never seen. It was becoming difficult finding places to put them and they were still being delivered to the back door. As fast as the flowers were coming, the line-up of girls checking in grew even more quickly. Anne was getting stressed with the demands of the girls and frustrated in finding space for the flowers, heart-shaped boxes of chocolates, teddy bears, balloons and baskets of fruit and nuts.

As Anne checked in Nicole she told her there were five arrangements of flowers for her. Nicole laughed and said, "You seem a little snowed under, Mom. Haven't you ever worked a Valentine's night before?"

"No, this is a first," Anne said. "I thought the girls would be spending this night with their significant others. Knowing most of the girls have husbands or boyfriends or in some cases both, I thought it would be a slow night."

"Oh no, Mom, not tonight. This is big, maybe even bigger than Mother's Day. Oh, yeah, these guys take their girlfriends or wives out to a fancy dinner, buy them a trinket and then make up some excuse to get away and they come here. This is going to be a great money night, so brace yourself. By the time this night is over there won't be a spot to put all the flowers and other stuff. It's a party."

The flowers kept arriving and so did the dancers. The shift had barely started and already a hundred and twenty-five girls had checked in. The Occupancy Permit, which was thumbtacked on a wall in the club, allowed for a thousand people: seven hundred and fifty customers, two hundred and fifty dancers. Anne was sure that number would be exceeded at the rate the girls were arriving. It would be hard to turn them away.

Eva checked in and Anne pointed to two gorgeous ruby red crystal vases brimming over with sterling silver roses that she had placed on her desk. "Those are for you, Eva," Anne said.

Eva reached for the card and, after reading it, tossed it into the trash. Turning to Anne she said, "I have no idea who this Dave is. I have three regulars with that name so I guess I will have to be very crafty in finding out which one sent the flowers. I'll figure it out, I always do. But I must say they are beautiful."

She leaned over and smelled the flowers. "Do you like them, Mom? Why don't you take them home? My boyfriend would never let me bring them into the house. He has no problem with me bringing jewelry and money home that I get from my customers but he has a real problem when it comes to flowers. I wonder why that is?"

Anne felt as if she had been working for hours when she took a quick look at the clock and realized it was just after ten o'clock. In three hours she had checked in two hundred girls and knew only fifty more would be able to work, when Frankie crashed into the Dressing Room.

"How many girls do we have so far?" he shouted.

"There's no need to shout, Frankie, you're standing right next to me. We have two hundred girls, which means I can only sign in fifty more according to the Occupancy Permit."

"Fuck that. Any stripper who comes through that door can work. Those permit rules don't apply to us. The fire commissioner is in here all the time; he doesn't care. Bring them all in. Every stripper that checks in means another ten dollars in my pocket. That means, so far I have a guaranteed two thousand dollar tip from the club, add that to what the girls tip me and it's going to be a very lucrative night for Frankie."

He reached into his pocket and pulled out an envelope.

"This is for you. I'll bet my club tips it's the only valentine you get."

Anne cautiously opened the envelope. Inside was a heart-shaped valentine card with a message Frankie had written. "Roses are red, Violets are blue, Sugar is sweet but you're not, so take this money and buy yourself something that will sweeten you up." Attached was five hundred dollars.

Anne laughed out loud and told Frankie how original he was and that she didn't know he cared. Frankie just smiled. He didn't get it. Walking away with a "mission accomplished" attitude, he held the purple door open for five dancers who told him they were leaving. They handed him several bills and then checked out with Anne.

Five were leaving, which meant Anne could check in fifty-five girls. She would keep careful track of those coming and going and perhaps she wouldn't go over the limit. If the fire department did do a check and the club was over the limit, it would be her head and not Frankie's.

By the end of the shift three hundred and seventy girls had checked in, and flowers and gifts covered every inch of the Dressing Room. Each girl would look at the card, toss it away and tell Anne she could have the gift, so Anne asked Marco, the night porter, to load every blossom, gift and box of chocolates into her car. The next morning she took the balloons and stuffed teddy bears to the Children's Hospital and the flowers and chocolates to a Hospice that was not far from her home, where they were graciously received and appreciated. As she drove away she wondered if the gifts would have been accepted if she had told them they came from a bunch of strippers.

She remembered the time a young family had lost everything in a house fire. The girls got together and raised three thousand dollars for them. When they presented the money to the wife, she refused the gift because it was from strippers. The husband looked very sheepish and said nothing. He was a regular at the club.

CHAPTER 59

Anne had the next three days off and was looking forward to just hanging out and recharging her batteries. She poured herself a glass of chilled Chardonnay and was just about to settle in with a good book when her phone rang.

In a gravelly voice Stella said, "Anne, I have one of the girls here who insists that I give her your phone number. She says it is really important that she talk to you, although I doubt that. She shouldn't be bothering you at home. I'm not giving it to her. Do you want to talk to her?"

"Of course, I'll talk to her."

Anne could hear Stella passing the phone to the dancer and telling her not to be long, this was a business phone.

"Mom, this is Mia. Sorry for bothering you at home but I can't wait until you come to work to tell you that I just got engaged! I'm getting married and I want you to be the mother of the bride."

"Congratulations, Mia! I am very happy for you, but can we talk about this when I come to work?"

"Perfect, Mom, perfect. I can hardly wait to see you."

Anne put her book down, picked up her glass of wine and thought about Mia. She was a petite Thai girl with the signature thick, jet-black hair down to her waist and she couldn't have weighed more than a hundred pounds. From the beginning she attached herself to Anne, telling her about her tragic past.

"It was really rough," Anne remembered Mia saying. "When I was seven years old my parents were killed in a car accident. There was no one to take care of me so I was placed in an orphanage. I worked in the kitchen, cooking and cleaning ten hours a day. My hands and knees were raw from scrubbing the floors. And despite the fact that I have spent a fortune on lotions and potions to soften them, nothing works. That's why I always wear lacy gloves when dancing. Three years later an American couple came to the orphanage looking to adopt a little girl. I was very nervous when I met them. Well, to make a long story short they adopted me and brought me to America. That was twelve years ago."

Anne had all the personal information on the girls and knew Mia was older than twenty-two.

"My father is an Irishman with deep blue yes, just like yours. He's six foot three. My mom was from France and she tried to teach me French but I was having enough trouble with English. My English still isn't very good. A couple of years after they adopted me, they divorced and she returned to France. I stayed here with my father."

That was her story.

When Anne returned to work, Mia was waiting for her. Mia grabbed and hugged her and launched into the details of her plans.

"Oh, Mia, you're going to have to wait a few minutes while I get set up for the evening," Anne said as she started to unpack the dinner she had prepared for the girls. Mia stepped up and began helping while talking non-stop, but she kept dropping things in her haste to help. Anne laughed, sat her down on a chair and told her not to talk or move until she was finished. When everything was in place, Anne said, "Now tell me your plans."

"We are being married next month at the Wedding Bell Chapel just off the Strip. I want you to be the mother of the bride. You won't have to do a thing, just show up."

"What about your own mother? Wouldn't she want to be at your wedding?"

Mia had a blank look on her face and started stumbling over her words. "My mother? Oh, she died a long time ago. My father will be there to give me away and he is looking forward to meeting you," she said with a wink. "Now, I've got to get to work, I have a wedding to pay for."

Over the next few weeks Anne and Mia shopped for the perfect wedding dress, and the invitations were chosen, addressed and mailed. The reception was to be held at a local Thai restaurant with a one-hundred-and-twenty-item buffet. Everything was in place when the day arrived.

Anne had chosen a knee-length, silk floral print dress for the occasion. She pulled her hair back in a knot, which showed off the diamond earrings Philip had given her on their wedding day. A matching wrap around her shoulders completed the outfit.

Refusing the offer of a limousine to pick her up, she drove to the chapel and parked in the designated area for guests. She walked up the white carpet to the entrance and opened the door. A bustle of energy met her.

"Thank goodness you're here, Mom," Sunny, the bridesmaid, said as she pinned an orchid corsage on Anne's right shoulder. As they made their way across the crowded reception area a tall, handsome man stepped forward.

"You have to be Anne," he said. "I'm Nelson, Mia's father for the evening. It's a pleasure to meet you."

Anne thought "father for the evening" was a strange thing to say. She shook his hand and said, "I am very happy for your daughter. She is a lovely young woman and I hope she and Jim will have a good life together."

Nelson took Anne by the arm and escorted her into the chapel. When she was seated, he smiled at her and excused himself.

The groom and his groomsman waited anxiously at the altar for the bride as the music started and Mia entered the chapel on the arm of her father, Nelson.

She was a vision in an ankle-length silk dress in the palest shade of pink, and her waist-length, glossy, black hair was adorned with a circle of baby pink roses, the same as her bouquet. At the altar Nelson kissed his daughter on the cheek and returned to his seat next to Anne.

After a short ceremony, everyone gathered outside chatting while the photographer took dozens and dozens of pictures of the bride and groom and their attendants. The limousine pulled up to take the wedding party to the reception and Anne headed for her car. Nelson stopped her.

"Would you mind if I drove with you? I'm not much for limousines and it will give us a chance to talk."

"Of course, come along. I will be happy for the company."

During the drive Nelson told Anne about his import/export business in Thailand and how he spent half his time there and the other half in California.

"It's a good life and I enjoy the traveling but it won't be the same now that Mia is married. She would often come with me, four or five times a year. The trips were never boring with her along. That woman can shop. I will miss her."

Anne turned on her right signal and turned into the restaurant's parking lot.

"Goodness, that was the fastest thirty minutes, and I did all the talking. Look, Anne, I'm going to be in town for the next couple of days, is there any chance that we could have dinner?"

Anne enjoyed his company and accepted his invitation. They agreed to meet at the Terminal Club at 7:00 pm the following evening. It was a very exclusive club with members being presidents of major companies and membership was by invitation only. It would be a nice change to be in a room with successful men, unlike the men she worked with. She had never been to the Terminal Club and looked forward to seeing if it was as grand as advertised.

She decided to wear a short, sleeveless, V-neck, black cocktail dress and her pearl necklace and earrings, another gift from Philip. As she clasped the pearls around her neck, she wondered how he was and if he was happy.

"Why am I thinking of him?" she thought. "I'm looking forward to an evening with a bright, handsome, charming and articulate man."

Anne drove up the winding driveway to the club, which was lined with lighted whitewashed palm trees, and pulled into the lane marked Visitors. Instantly, a young man in uniform opened her car door. On telling him her name, he told her Mr. Strand would come for her momentarily. He walked her to the main entrance and within seconds Nelson was at her side.

"You look beautiful," he said as he offered her his arm and they ascended the wide marble staircase to the main foyer. At the top of the stairs and to the right Anne saw several couples dancing. She paused for a moment. Nelson followed her gaze, took her by the hand and led her to the dance floor. She fit perfectly in his arms as they moved to the music. Anne told him he was a marvelous dancer and he replied, "It's pretty easy when I have a partner like you."

They left the dance floor and were escorted to their table by the maître d', who had greeted them with the utmost of respect. Anne figured the Terminal Club was Nelson's home away from home.

Their table was by a window that looked over a glorious garden where couples were gathered celebrating a wedding. Nelson told her it was the wedding of one of the members.

"I suggested to Mia that she might like to have her wedding here but she wouldn't have anything to do with that. She came here with me several times but never felt comfortable. I could never understand why because it is a very discreet, friendly club."

Anne knew why. There were several members of this club who were regulars at another club.

Nelson ordered a rare bottle of wine and when the wine was poured they toasted the bride and groom. Sitting back in his chair,

Nelson said in a very sad voice, "It was strange indeed, giving my ex-wife away yesterday to another man."

Anne almost choked on her wine. "Mia is your ex-wife?"

"Yes. I met her about ten years ago on one of my many trips to Thailand. I remember so clearly walking into the Platinum Club, which is a very high-end exotic dance club and there she was on center stage. I was captivated the moment I laid eyes on her. She danced for me in the VIP room and before the first dance was over I was planning my next trip back. I made many trips for several years showering her with money and jewelry and I bought her an apartment. I was spending too much time there and my business was suffering so I asked her to marry me and move to the States.

The waiter was at their table to take their order. Anne had lost all interest in dinner, fascinated with Nelson's story. He ordered a Caesar salad and rare filet of beef for both of them, and then continued his story.

"She had no issue with the twenty-five-year age difference and she really wanted to move to the States but she told me she was supporting her parents who lived in a little village outside of Bangkok and they were wholly dependent on her financially. So, I set up an account for her folks and sent money each month. We were married and the long process and stacks of paperwork began for her to immigrate. I knew it would take time and I asked her not to continue dancing but she did. She had her own agenda. Finally, after months and months she was cleared to come to California. It was wonderful having her here and she adapted quickly but the language was a problem."

The waiter came to their table and topped up their wine.

"I arranged for a tutor to come to the house daily," Nelson went on, "and within weeks her English improved. She is a very smart woman but she was getting bored and soon insisted on going to work. She went back to dancing. I was very disappointed but as long as she was happy, that's all I cared about.

"We were married seven years when she told me she had met Jim. He was one of her customers, a lawyer, who was being transferred to Vegas and she wanted to go with him. I was devastated but I let her go. We were divorced forty-five days ago."

The waiter came and cleared away their dinner plates, which were barely touched, and asked if they would like anything else.

Nelson ordered coffee and Courvoisier.

"They leave on their honeymoon tomorrow. Did you know they're going to Thailand to visit her parents? Seems her parents are schoolteachers in that little village and fairly well off. Before coming to the States, Mia sold her apartment and bought her parents a house. She is a smart girl, smarter than me. Do old fools ever learn, Anne? But I'd do it all again."

The waiter brought the check for Nelson's signature and they left the club. He walked her to her car.

"I have to go to Thailand within the week and will be gone for two months. When I return could I see you again?" he asked. He bent down and kissed her on the cheek.

A month later, Mia called Anne. Her father had suffered a massive heart attack and died. She sounded very upset, but in the same breath told Anne he had left everything to her. She would not be returning to work because she was expecting her first child and she and her husband would be going to Thailand to take over her father's business.

Anne thought a lot about Mia over the next few days. She thought about a young woman who felt compelled to rewrite her history. She can hide her past but she will always know the truth.

CHAPTER 60

Frankie pushed open the purple door, screaming for Aqua. He made his way toward Anne's desk, limping, with a pained look on his face. It was clear the new python cowboy boots were giving him trouble.

"Where is the bitch? Find her, get her, bring her to me. I'm going to kill her," he demanded of Anne.

"She left," one of the girls said as she made her way into the club.

"Why the hell did you let her go? You have no idea the damage she has caused. Thousands and thousands of dollars and she will pay for it if I ever get my hands on her. The club will have to close to clean up the mess she made. When the owner finds out he will fire all of us."

"What in the world could she have done to get you so upset?" Anne said.

"That stupid bitch was swinging her black ass all over the stage when she decided to try swinging from the water pipes. You know, they run along the stage and have since this place was built, God knows how long ago. Who but Aqua could even reach the fuckin' pipes? Bare feet she's six feet tall, add the shoes and you can do the math. She just reached up and grabbed a hold. Within seconds the pipes broke and the water came gushing out. It's rolling off the stage. I saw the whole damn thing happen right before my eyes. It's crazy out there. Three poles on stage weren't enough for her. Hell, no, she had to reach for the pipes. The water is everywhere, customers getting soaked, screaming they're gonna sue. Why the hell would she swing from the pipes? I don't get it. The carpet and chairs are soaked, some of the electrical circuits have blown and the water just keeps pouring out. I don't know what to do?"

"Have you turned off the water?" Anne asked with a straight face.

"Oh, my God, I never thought of that."

He raced back into the club, almost tripping over his new custom boots with two-inch heels, boots that would almost get him up to five feet nine inches.

"Do you think they'll close the club, Mom? I have bills to pay, I have to work," Lana asked.

"Hell no," Charlie said before Anne could answer. "They will keep this sucker open no matter what. God forbid the old fart who owns this dump should lose a nickel. They'll get a cleanup crew in here and it will be business as usual. No worries there. This building is over fifty years old, what do they expect? Nothing has been done for years to fix it up, serves them right."

The girls were filing into the Dressing Room, wiping themselves and their shoes with bar towels.

"That lousy bartender, we had to tip him twenty bucks for a couple of these ratty towels. God, he takes advantage of us," Sandy said as she threw the towels in the trash.

"What's happening out there?" someone asked.

"Business as usual. Frankie finally caught a brain and turned the water off but it took him a long time. He didn't know where the switch-off valve was and came to find out it's up on the roof. The bouncers found a rickety old ladder out back and they held it and Frankie climbed up. He found the valve and got the water turned off but at the same time he lost his footing and fell off the roof, and a lot of old tiles came down with him. He's pretty banged up. Couldn't happen to a nicer guy," Cathy said.

CHAPTER 61

"Is the club all fixed up?" Crystal asked as she checked in. "I came early hoping to get a couple more hours of work in but the parking lot is almost empty. I missed three nights' work because of Aqua, but if you stop and think about it, she did us a favor; they finally had no choice but to clean up this place. It sure smells better."

Crystal was the young dancer on center stage when Anne came for her interview. She remembered the beauty of her tanned, chiseled body as she made her way up to the top of the pole. She was the club's top money maker.

"How do you like being a House Mom, Mom?" Crystal asked. "It's probably very different from what you did before. Most of the girls and other House Moms didn't think you would last because this is a rough business and you're such a lady, but you sure fooled them."

She handed Anne her Sheriff's Card.

"It wouldn't be so bad if some of the girls would take this job seriously; so many of the weekenders just come to have a party. Some just don't get it and others think all they need is a set of thirty-eight double D's and they've got it made, but it takes more than that to make the really big money. I hear them complaining to the customers about how they're not making any money. Some even get a crying jag going on hoping to get sympathy from the guy and he'll give up the money, but that only works for so long.

"You've got to know how to strut your stuff and use body language and at the same time watch the customer's body language, it speaks volumes — body language — the way a dancer walks in her stilettos, how she sits down, how she holds her liquor. There is nothing worse than a drunken woman. That is so gross. Some don't even know how to approach a guy. You've got to introduce yourself, shake the guy's hand and smile, smile, smile. Make him feel like he's the only customer in the club. You might not get a dance but some other guy across the room may have been observing you. He sees that you leave people smiling and you yourself are smiling. Ten to one, he will seek you out for a dance or better still, a VIP."

Several girls were at the door buzzing to get in. Crystal continued talking while Anne checked the dancers in and collected the tip-out.

"Some guys are really intimidated by a beautiful woman, but when they see how friendly you are, it makes it easier for them to come up and ask for a dance. But of course, you get the most attention with your stage work. When I'm on stage I own that stage, it's mine and I know I give the best stage performance of any dancer in this club. I work out with a personal trainer three times a week so I have a lot of strength in my upper body but the older I get the harder it is to maintain."

She stopped talking for a second and pulled a chair up to Anne's desk.

"When I was a kid my parents enrolled me in a gymnastics school and I loved it. My coach was convinced I would be an Olympic contender and I might have been if my parents hadn't divorced. It was a struggle for Mom raising me with no support whatsoever from Dad. He took off with a younger woman and left Mom high and dry. He falls into the category of the dead-beat dad. It broke Mom's heart when I couldn't continue with my training, but it wasn't a total loss. All that training, discipline and hard work makes me a lot of money and that money is putting me through university. Mom hates the fact that I dance."

Crystal laughed to herself.

"Life is funny. Before Mom met my father she was studying to be a ballet dancer but when she became pregnant with me she had to give it up. But she never lost her passion for it. My goal is to set her up in her own studio where she can teach ballet to children. I told her whenever she is ready, it will happen, and I will make it happen. She wants to wait until I graduate from university. That is her number one passion now, to see me graduate."

"What are you studying?" Anne asked.

"Special Education. I want to work with children. Teach them gymnastics and get involved with the Olympics. Maybe I will have my own contender one day. I didn't make it, but maybe I can help someone who will."

Anne's telephone was ringing and she reached for it. It was Frankie wanting to know if Crystal had checked in. One of her regular customers, Mr. D., was in the club. Anne relayed the message to Crystal.

"Thank my lucky stars. What I lost the three days I didn't work, this guy will make up a hundred-fold in a few hours, and it won't be a late night for me. See you later."

Crystal was on her way into the club when the purple door opened. She held it for two dancers who were helping Tanis.

"We need some help here, Mom."

Anne made her way around the desk and helped them get Tanis into a chair. She was pretty banged up; both elbows and knees were scraped and bleeding. Anne reached for her first aid kit and started cleaning her up. She couldn't do much to help her swollen eye, which was already turning black and blue, except have her hold an ice bag to it. She was very intoxicated. The girls got her a cup of strong black coffee.

"We told her not to go on stage and we also asked the DJ not to put her on stage, even tipped him a twenty but he didn't listen. He was too busy snorting to pay much attention to anyone. She had so much to drink and I'll bet money the rotten bartender put something in her drink. She was on stage doing her routine but moving too fast and not paying attention. She reached out to swing around the third pole but it's gone. She flew off the stage like Peter Pan and landed in the lap of a customer. Her elbow caught him in the eye. Frankie is out there feeding the guy free drinks hoping he gets so drunk he won't remember how he got the shiner. God only knows where her shoes are, they flew in two different directions."

Tanis looked up, on the verge of tears.

"No one told me they took away the pole. Why didn't Frankie tell me about the missing pole? That's not right."

"If you weren't so drunk you would have noticed the pole was gone, you stupid bitch. They took the pole away when Aqua took down the water pipes," the other two dancers cried.

"There's no need to be calling her names. She has been through enough," Anne said.

"Ah, we know, Mom, but she doesn't listen. Tanis never drank until she started dancing and we've told her time and time again to lay off the booze. It just started as a casual, fun thing for her but it has now become a crutch. She says she can't work without having some drinks, it makes it easier for her to deal with some of the scummy guys, but she takes it over the edge. I told her if she had to get drunk to do her job then she should think about a career change. Take a look at her ankle, it's swelling up. She won't be able to dance for a week."

"I'm fine," Tanis slurred. "Stop fussing over me, I'm going back to work. Where are my fuckin' shoes?"

"Those shoes are long gone," her friend said. "Some creep out there has found them and will probably sleep with them tonight, just like that crazy Chuck who comes in here wanting to buy our old shoes." She turned to Anne and explained, "As long as the shoe has an imprint of our foot he'll give us a hundred bucks for them. That sick son-of-a-bitch has a foot fetish. You're shoes are long gone, Tanis. Mom, will you call us a cab, I've got to get her home."

No sooner had Anne got the dancers in the cab, when Crystal came back.

"Mr D. has left the building," she said. "He's in town for a fund-raiser and his wife is with him this trip. He had to leave to pick her up for dinner. That doesn't happen often. He's been my regular for the past three years. Flies down here from Seattle every couple of weeks and always leaves me with ten thousand dollars. He gave me five to-night but he'll be back tomorrow. It's not often I ever dance for him; we just sit and talk mainly about him. He pours his heart out to me about his marriage and spoiled kids, but when he talks about his business I pay very close attention. He's involved big time in an internet company and is a very wealthy man.

"Two years ago I bought a thousand shares of his company's stock and that stock is worth ten times more today."

She reached behind her and placed a velvet box on Anne's desk.

"He gave this to me before he left. It's from Tiffany's and if you don't mind recycled gifts, I'd like to give it to you, Mom."

Anne opened the box and inside was an eighteen-karat gold chain with a two-ounce gold pendant.

"Do you like it, Mom? It's one of their signature pieces."

"It's beautiful, Crystal, thank you."

"I'm glad you like it, every girl should have something from Tiffany's. Now I'm going to call it a night."

CHAPTER 62

After Crystal left, Anne thought about the dinner party she had attended the month before with guests who seemed to outdo each other with their Tiffany jewelry. She didn't know many of the guests except Rick and Janet, the host and hostess, and as she was introduced the introduction was always followed with "Anne is a lawyer." They were polite with their questions regarding what field of law, what firm she worked for, the usual chatter. Anne made it very clear that she no longer practised law but worked in an exotic topless dance club as a House Mom. There was no lack of conversation from that moment on. The women, most of whom were dressed in the little black dress with the perennial string of Tiffany pearls, were very curious.

"Why, I've never heard of such a job," one of the women said. "How did you ever get involved with a strip club? What are the strippers like, are they all prostitutes on drugs?" Anne found their ignorance sad but at the same time amusing.

Janet interrupted the conversation with a tray of tiger prawns, with a crystal bowl of cocktail sauce in the center. The women thanked her and said they found Anne's new career fascinating.

"Oh, when she gets bored with the sleazy world of strippers, she will return to the practice of law," Janet said.

Anne laughed.

"Janet, what could be sleazier than the practice of law? The dancers are more honest about their work than any lawyer I've ever worked with. They have no illusions of why they have chosen stripping to earn a living and have no problem separating fact from fiction.

They know why they dance. They come to work, get in, do their job, make their money and go home and they don't take their jobs home with them."

"That's what you say now," Janet said, "but I know you will come to your senses and go back to law. Now, let's join the men and see what they are up to."

Anne knew she had upset her friend. They had met during their high school years and had remained in touch ever since. Back then Janet's goal was to marry a professional man, have the big house, two kids, two cars and the picket fence. She certainly obtained her goal. Rick was a shrewd, powerful litigator and senior partner in a top law firm. Janet's reason for existing was to keep him happy. She was the ultimate of hostesses and as far as she was concerned an excellent mother, although Anne wondered why an excellent mother shipped her two children off to a private boarding school in Switzerland.

They entered the room and the men turned, each holding a martini in one hand and a Cuban cigar in the other.

"What have you girls been up to?" Rick asked. "Solving all the world's problems?"

Janet sidled up to Rick and put her arm through his and looked up at him. "Oh, nothing so grand. Anne was just giving the ladies a rundown on her new job."

"How is that going for you, Anne? Quite removed from your previous job I dare say."

"What does she do?" Jack, a partner in one of the biggest law firms in Los Angeles, asked as he adjusted his dinner jacket in an attempt to hide the pot belly that hung over his belt, ignoring the fact that Anne was standing right in front of him.

"She works in a strip joint," Rick replied.

"A strip joint, good God. What possesses men to go to those places and throw away their hard-earned cash? You would never find me in one of those places," the pot-bellied guest said.

"The guys who frequent strip clubs must be real hard up for female company. Those women are the losers of the world with a capital L. They come into the office wanting us to get them off a DUI or any number of things. I've never dealt with them, I just hand them over to a junior, but I know what goes on in those clubs. I have knowledge."

Anne took a couple of steps closer to him and smiled.

"If you have never been a patron at a strip club, as you say, then you are basing your perception of exotic dancers on what the media wants you to believe and because of that, the knowledge that you say you have needs to be questioned."

Several of the women stepped closer and stood at Anne's side.

"For a lawyer as bright as you that's quite surprising to me," Anne continued, "so let me set you straight, Sonny Boy. The dancers are not losers, just women earning a living. If you ever ventured into a strip club just once you would return many times, I guarantee it. Where can a man go and be made to feel like the most important person in the world by a beautiful woman who is dressed in a very sexy outfit and whose only objective is to make you feel special. She may stand in front of you swaying her perfect body and dance for you. She will lightly touch your hair, your shoulders and tell you how handsome you are and sit on your knee and listen while you talk about yourself. You will tell her that you're married but your wife doesn't understand you. Ah, but the beauty sitting on your knee understands. She will look with sympathetic baby blue eyes into yours believing everything you tell her."

Anne took a step closer and noticed sweat was already forming on his brow.

"She doesn't nag you, question why you're getting home late, why you have to work so much. She knows that is your real world and she takes you out of it with her natural sexuality, her creativity, her flirtatious spirit in making you feel comfortable, and believe me, by the time she finishes cooing in your ear all the things your wife doesn't coo, she will have you eating out of her hand. You will leave her with a thousand dollars or more, telling her it's a gift. You will ask her what nights she works because you know you will be back. On the drive home to your wife and kids, you will think about her while pulling at your crotch, both your heads in a sexual mode, planning on when you can get back to see her again. You're hooked. You say you have knowledge; having it and understanding it are two different things."

"Dinner is served," the hostess said.

The dinner conversation centered on homeland security and what the US President was doing to keep America safe. Nothing, was the general consensus, and every man sitting at that table believed he could do a better job running the country. Talk was cheap. Anne said little, as was her policy when talk turned to politics or religion.

After dinner, Natasha, one of the guests approached her. She was a beautiful woman in her mid-thirties, Anne guessed, tall, at least five foot eight. Her shoulder-length blonde hair had a two-hundred-dollar hair cut and her royal blue designer dress came just slightly above her knees, revealing a pair of legs that anyone would admire. She was picture perfect.

"I'm very curious about your job, it interests me," Natasha started. "How does one become a stripper and what qualifications are required? Is it true they make a lot of money?"

Anne and Natasha picked up their after-dinner coffee and made their way to a corner to sit down.

"Yes, they do make a lot of money but they work hard for it," Anne explained. "Dancing is not an easy life. You have to have very tough skin to make it and a lot of street smarts. Being in good physical shape is important; the work takes a terrific toll on the body. So many girls have back problems, their knees and ankles grow weak because of the stilettos and their feet certainly suffer. Great looks and a great body are important, but you also have to have personality and be able to carry on an intelligent conversation to make the big money."

"Where do you work?"

"The Tiger Club," Anne said as Natasha's husband came looking for her with her wrap over his arm.

"It's time to go, we have a plane to catch," he said.

Anne shook hands with Natasha and said it was a pleasure meeting her and perhaps one day they would meet again. Natasha's friend, Sylvie, came over to them. Natasha put her arm around her friend and told Anne they had been friends since high school.

"What were you and Anne talking about?" Anne heard Sylvie ask Natasha as they were leaving.

"I'll tell you tomorrow over coffee."

Anne believed there was more going on in this lady's pretty head than mere curiosity.

CHAPTER 63

Anne was on the road early running errands. Her last stop was the grocery store. As she parked her car, a white Mercedes SUV pulled in next to her. The driver looked over at her and smiled. It was Shelly.

"What a nice surprise running into you, Anne. Is it okay if I call you Anne?" Shelly asked.

"Of course, call me Anne. I was just finishing my to-do list and grocery shopping is my last stop, but I was thinking I would like a double latte before tackling that job. Do you have time to join me?"

"Yes, I would like that."

They walked to the coffee shop together, ordered their lattes and settled in comfy chairs.

"Do you live in the area?" Shelly asked. "I'm at King's Cross, not too far from here."

"Yes, I do, and I'm just a few blocks west of King's Cross. It's a beautiful area and I like living here."

"Are you surprised that a stripper would live in such an elite area?"

"Heavens, no, quite the contrary, I would think a lot of girls live in this area because they can certainly afford the real estate. Have you lived here long?"

"Five years. I remember when King's Cross was being built and I would tell myself that someday I would live there. I dreamt big back then because at that time I was homeless, along with my mother and two younger sisters. It was tough after my father left. He was a truck driver, on the road a lot and rarely at home. Mom worked as a waitress until she had us kids. There was never enough money and they fought constantly when he was home, and then one time he just didn't come back."

She took a sip of her latte.

"I haven't seen him for years and often wonder where he is and if he ever thinks about the kids he left behind. Mom went back to waitressing, but we were always one check away from being homeless and that eventually happened. About six months later she met a man at the casino where she worked and he swept her off her feet. Within days he moved us into an apartment and it felt like we had a home again. Mom was very happy, but I didn't like him because he smoked pot. Mom never did drugs but soon she was joining him and before long they were into the hard stuff. It wasn't long after that she lost her job. And just like my father before, one day he just didn't come home."

The double lattes were gone and Anne ordered two cups of decaf coffee. Shelly continued.

"I was just shy of my eighteenth birthday and a month from graduating high school. I always dreamed of going to college but when I turned eighteen I applied at the Tiger Club. At that time you only had to be eighteen years old to dance. When I started I had nothing, not even shoes. There was a dancer who took me under her wing by loaning me costumes and giving me a pair of shoes. She was a university student who worked weekends and I could hardly wait for the weekends when she would come to work. She was very good to me and I see a lot of her in you, and maybe that's why I am so drawn to you."

Memories floated back to Anne.

"After my first week I had enough money to move all of us into a two-bedroom apartment. We had a real roof over our heads and food in the fridge. I got my sisters enrolled in the local school and they did well. Kelly, who is now twenty-three years old, is a dental hygienist and Sandy, who is twenty-one, is finishing her last year in design school.

"I gave Kelly the down payment for her townhouse and I told Sandy I would do the same for her when she graduated. I am very proud of them.

"I convinced Mom to go into rehab and she seems to have her act together, but it's hard for me to trust her. She took an accounting course and works for a casino on the Strip."

Anne sat quietly listening to Shelly's story, and she was humbled. She asked, "What about you, Shelly? What are your dreams?"

"This is not how I would have drawn my life, Anne. No young girl grows up wanting to be a stripper. I had dreams of writing the great American novel but I have been in the business for so long that I will continue as long as this body holds up. I have made a lot of money over the years and have investments that will keep me in my old age. I rather doubt anyone is going to come along and keep me in my twilight years. I've met few men who are worth my time."

She looked at her watch.

"Oh, gosh, look at the time. I'm sorry Anne, I just keep babbling along. I don't know how I got into all this but it seems so easy to talk to you. You are an amazing woman."

"You're the amazing one, Shelly."

They said goodbye and went their separate ways.

CHAPTER 64

"He's back. He's sitting in the upper VIP section. Stay clear of that area at all costs," Molly said as she came into the Dressing Room. "Frankie is over there fawning all over the son-of-a-bitch, giving the wild animal free drinks and telling him to pick any girl he wants and Frankie will make it happen."

"Who are you talking about?" Anne asked.

"The worse guy in the world. He's huge, stands at least six foot seven and must weigh at least two hundred and ninety pounds. He makes his living with his fists, the super star, the jock that gets his kicks out of beating up and raping women. He hasn't been here for awhile, not since he punched Dahlia and knocked her to the ground. That was a terrible night."

Frankie came into the Dressing Room wanting to know how many girls had checked in. He looked around and took note of who was there before he left.

Molly continued her story.

"Dahlia was just finishing her shift, ready to check out when the jock spotted her. He hollered to her but she ignored him. Frankie, seeing what was happening, stopped her and begged her to go sit with the guy for a few minutes and do a dance.

"He told Dahlia that if she did him this favor, he'd take care of her and wouldn't charge her the house tip-out for a week.

"Dahlia went along with him to meet the goon. When he saw her walking toward him he stood up. This was unusual for him because he didn't stand for anybody, he expected everybody to bow to him. I noticed all this and thought something wasn't right, what is he going to do? Before you could blink an eye he pulled back his fist and slammed it into her face. She fell down and then he kicked her in the back screaming that no fuckin' white bitch ignored him. It happened so fast. The bouncers carried her to the Dressing Room and the paramedics were called. He did some serious damage to her back, broke her hose and injured her eye.

"Fortunately, Dr. Chan was here and we got a couple of Vicodin for her while we waited for the ambulance. Ten minutes after the whole thing went down, things were back to normal. Frankie said she couldn't come back to work. She was wrong for ignoring the jock, you didn't ignore someone as important as the man who was a world champ, and the rest of the girls had better take a lesson from this. When a big name is in the club, he is to be catered to, don't ignore the jock."

Anne sat back in her chair, astonished.

"About a month later Dahlia went to see Phil, a good lawyer, and a lawsuit was filed against the club, Frankie, the bouncers and the super jock. When all the witnesses were questioned, it turned out they all had short-term memory loss except for me and another girl. After weeks and weeks, it was finally settled out of court. Frankie said he would have fired me and the other girls if it had gone to court. Dahlia got a lot of money, thanks to her lawyer, but she will have problems for the rest of her life. She is dancing at another club and is doing okay but she sure can't dance the way she used to. We always let the new girls know about this monster."

Frankie came through the purple door twirling a key chain around his index finger announcing the super jock was in the house and the girls were to be at his beck and call. As a matter of fact, he needed a couple of girls to do some dances for him right now. No one volunteered.

"C'mon, he's harmless," Frankie said. "Look I need someone to dance for him and I'll give five hundred dollars to anyone who will have a drink with him and do a dance. Just one dance. We're only talking about fifteen minutes of your time."

Holly stepped up.

"Okay, Frankie, I'll go but I want the five hundred dollars up front and a bouncer within two feet of me."

He peeled off five one-hundred-dollar bills and handed them to her but he knew that five hundred would get him a thousand from super jock. As Holly was leaving to go into the club, Molly called her back.

"Be careful out there and make sure you come back with everything you left with."

Nobody laughed because they knew this was no laughing matter.

Thirty minutes later there was no sign of her and Anne was getting very concerned. Molly went to check and as she opened the purple door two bouncers were walking toward her holding up Holly.

"Oh, my God, what did he do?" Molly asked as she reached for her friend. Holly was holding her breasts and it was obvious she was in a great deal of pain. Anne rushed to her and said she would call the paramedics, but Holly stopped her.

"No, Mom, don't call the medics. Call my husband, Ron, he'll come and get me."

Anne held an ice bag to Holly's enormous breasts; breasts that would make the Grand Canyon look like a ditch. Swelling black and blue marks were already appearing on her chest.

"I shouldn't have ignored him while I was dancing. I was thinking of my two little girls and what we would do tomorrow, my day off. The scumbag was so fast. He grabbed my breasts in his dirty hands and twisted as hard as he could. I dropped to my knees. I think the silicone sacs have busted. When my husband gets here, he'll take me to the hospital."

She was very composed considering the ordeal she had just been through, but when her husband showed up she fell apart. She kept apologizing to him, crying and saying over and over how sorry she was and even sorrier that she only made a thousand dollars.

"Is he still in the club?" Ron asked. "I'll kill him. I'll take the bastard down. A thousand bucks is nothing, you should be coming home with at least two thousand."

Frankie came into the Dressing Room and, seeing Ron, he extended his hand and patted him on the back. Ron demanded to know why Frankie and his boys weren't watching out for his wife.

"That's their job, isn't it, Frankie? I know how much my wife tips them every night and for what? They sure fucked up tonight."

"Yeah, it's pretty awful what he did and he's really sorry. He hopes this will make up for it. This guy doesn't want another law suit." He handed Ron ten thousand dollars.

Ron took the money and stuffed it into his pants pocket.

"It's a damn good thing he gave me this money. Holly hasn't been making much lately and we need it. I just had a new sound system installed in my truck, a new chrome grill and rims. If she didn't insist the kids go to a private school we wouldn't have so damn many money problems."

He opened the door and Holly followed him out to his truck with the fancy new grill.

After they left, Molly said, "She'll get new boobs and be back to work in six weeks. Ron is nothing more than a pimp. I wish she would leave him but I guess any man is better than no man as far as she's concerned."

"Molly," Anne said, "you marry at the level of your own self-esteem. Holly believes Ron is all that she deserves."

CHAPTER 65

With a clipboard and pad of paper tucked under his arm and looking very officious, Frankie stood in the Dressing Room and looked
around. He paid no attention to Anne and even less to the girls, or
so it seemed. He jotted down numbers on the pad of paper, circling
the room several times, and he seemed quite proud of himself as he
walked over to Anne.

"How many girls do we have so far?" he asked as he tossed the
clipboard on Anne's desk.

"A hundred and ninety, Frankie," Anne said without looking up.

"Yeah, I figured it was around that. We'll probably get several dozen
more, is my guess. I hope we reach two hundred and fifty. That would
put twenty-five hundred dollars in my pocket. Not a bad Friday night's
tip. I wish the old man who owns this joint would pump it up to fifteen
dollars a girl. Hell, I'm worth it. The old geezer sails into the parking lot
in his chauffeured Silver Shadow, with his entourage, and walks into
the club as though he's God. He has more money than brains."

"Quite the opposite, Frankie, that old geezer, as you refer to him,
has used his brain to make a lot of money. Perhaps, you should think
about doing that yourself," Anne said. "Just a thought."

"You're real funny, Anne. Now, enough of that crap. I've got to get
back into the club and lighten it up. I've noticed its dark in here too,
so lighten it up."

He started to walk away.

"Too dark? What are you talking about? The lights are the same as they are every night. I don't understand how you want me to lighten up the Dressing Room."

"Don't get smart with me, Anne. I can have your job, you know. You may think you're smarter than me but you're not."

Several of the girls overhearing, laughed.

"I'm not talking about the Dressing Room," he said over his shoulder with a nasty smirk on his face as he disappeared into the club.

Anne forgot about Frankie and counted the tip-out that she had collected; so far the amount was twelve thousand three hundred and fifty dollars and the night wasn't over. Not too bad for one shift. She locked the cash drawer and was pouring herself a cup of coffee when the purple door was pushed open and slammed up against the wall as four dancers made their way to her, cussing to themselves.

"Frankie is sending us home. We can have our tip-out back. It's so unfair because I was just starting to make money. He's such a cockroach."

"Why is he sending you home?"

"Oh, c'mon Mom, you know as well as we do that Frankie wants to lighten up the joint, says it's too dark."

Anne's mouth dropped open.

"Are you telling me that when Frankie told me to lighten up the Dressing Room, he meant that I was not to check in any African-American dancers?"

"That's exactly what he meant," Shana said.

"That's ridiculous. I will check in every girl who comes through that door regardless of color."

"Don't do that, Mom. You'll just make it harder on the girls and yourself. Frankie will just send them home."

"He can't do that. That's discrimination, it's against the law."

The four girls laughed.

"There's only one law in this joint and that's Frankie's law. Now, if you give us back our house tip-out, we can get out of here and go to another club."

Anne returned the tip-out to the girls.

"Well, this night wasn't a complete loss," said Shana. "At least Dr. Chan is here and he gave me a prescription for Percocet. Wrote it out for a hundred this time, times that by six and that's six hundred dollars in my pocket, add that to the thousand that I made and I guess it isn't such a bad night."

"Yeah, he gave me a script for Vicodin but only made it for fifty. But I'll get five hundred for these dolls."

"Who is Dr. Chan?" Anne asked.

"He's a doctor who comes in here often," Shana said. "A dirty old man who will write a prescription for anything we want for the low price of a lap dance." She put the prescription in her purse.

"I don't do drugs. I guess it would be fun in the beginning but too soon you get addicted and you're doing more than just a dance on Dr. Chan's lap for that little piece of paper. I've seen it happen over and over in this club. It isn't going to happen to me."

"That is so wrong," Anne said.

"Are you talking about us being kicked out because we're black or because of this little side business we've got going on?"

"Both," Anne said.

CHAPTER 66

Friday night rolled around and it was going to be busy with another big convention in town. The weekenders were arriving earlier than usual and Frankie would be showing up around nine o'clock, no doubt wearing a new pair of cowboy boots. Anne hadn't seen much of him since the broken water pipe fiasco when he fell off the roof. It was a good joke among the girls until Frankie tried to put a stop to it when he found out they thought his falling was hysterical.

"Ah, we know it wasn't funny," they told him, "just the image."

He seemed to accept that as their way of apologizing but the story continued behind his back, getting more elaborate with each telling.

It was a little after ten o'clock when the purple door flew open and he pounded into the Dressing Room screaming like a demented beast with two bouncers following close behind. His jacket was off, shirt sleeves rolled up revealing arms covered in Tigers, his tie hanging loosely around his neck, sweaty armpits, his eyes filled with rage as he dragged Tia behind him.

The veins in his thick neck seemed ready to burst. His fat, chunky fingers encircled Tia's tiny arm as he threw her down on the floor. Bent over, his balled-up fists on his knees, he hollered insult upon insult as she lay in the fetal position with her long jet-black hair spilling over the linoleum floor. Her stilettos lay next to her petite four-foot-eleven frame. The two six-foot-three, steroid-induced bouncers leaned against the lockers, one cleaning his fingernails with a Swiss Army knife, both agreeing with every verbal abuse Frankie laid on Tia.

"Where's the money, you grimy little bitch," Frankie screamed, spittle flying out of his mouth.

"I didn't take it, I didn't take it!" Tia cried. She tried to get up but Frankie put his knee across her heaving chest to hold her down.

"The customer said you stole fifty bucks from him. I know you took it. Hand it over or I will knock the shit out of your miserable body."

The bouncers shifted position, the bald-headed one now polishing his fingernails against his shirt, while the other stared at a dancer getting dressed.

Frankie continued his tirade over the limp body, the purplish veins at his temple bulging, his face a deep crimson red. He moved closer to her and Tia could smell on his breath the grilled salmon dinner he'd just eaten.

"Give it over," he demanded.

Anne walked slowly from behind her desk over to Tia, the little dancer from the Philippines. The Dressing Room was silent with all eyes now on Anne. Without a word she reached down to pick her up.

Frankie turned, surprised to see Anne beside him. The loudness and tone of his voice didn't change.

"What the hell do you think you're doing? Get the hell back behind your desk where you belong. This is none of your fuckin' business."

Anne said nothing. She gently reached for the child-like woman and then felt the bouncer's hand on her upper arm.

"Don't interfere, Mom," he said.

"Take your hand off me and don't ever call me Mom."

He eased his hold but his hand remained on her arm. She brushed it off and turned to Tia, who was perfectly still, spent, tired and quietly sobbing.

"What's going on here?" asked the neon pink-clad cocktail waitress, Sally, between chaws on a wad of gum, a permanent fixture in her mouth. No rules for Sally.

"This bitch stole fifty bucks from a customer," Frankie said.

"Oh, do you mean the guy in the navy polyester leisure suit, the fat guy with the comb-over hairdo?" she asked with a laugh.

Frankie stood up, finding Sally's cash caddy of more interest than the dancer who was now being helped by Anne.

"That guy was out there hollering that he had been ripped off for fifty bucks. As I was putting a fresh drink down in front of him my eye caught a fifty-dollar bill on the floor."

She flipped open the cash caddy and waved the fifty-dollar bill in the air.

Frankie and the bouncers high-fived her. She handed a twenty to Frankie as they walked back into the club sharing the joke, forgetting about the damage done to Tia. As soon as Frankie and the bouncers left the Dressing Room, the girls rushed over.

"Is she going to be alright, Mom?" Why would we steal fifty bucks when we know we'll get at least two hundred from the guy. It doesn't make any sense."

Anne wrapped a soft blanket around Tia's shoulders and asked if she wanted to report this abuse.

"He assaulted you and left marks on your arms. He should be charged, and I will help you."

"I can't, Mom. I've got two little kids at home who depend on me. Their loser father is in jail. I'm all they have, and tomorrow Frankie will have forgotten all about this. I've got to go back to work."

"Do you have a daughter, Tia?" Anne asked.

Her eyes lit up.

"Yes, I do. Her name is Maria and she's seven years old going on twenty."

"How would you feel if a man treated her just the way Frankie treated you?"

"He'd be talking about it from behind bars, if I didn't kill him first."

"But you won't do it for yourself."

Tia looked at Anne. The tears were gone, the marks on her arm turning color. She picked up her shoes, hugged Anne and quietly walked away.

CHAPTER 67

Shelly burst through the purple door bent over with laughter and went to Anne.

"Lordy, lord! You should have seen Sherry in action tonight. She sure knows how to handle the new boys. She smoked this poor guy like a finely rolled cigar. She should be back any minute."

Anne waved her into a chair on the other side of her desk and said, "I'm intrigued, tell me more."

She flopped down and gathered bits of her costume around her.

"Picture this. A guy comes in by himself. He's looking really nervous and keeps pushing his hair back off his forehead. He's seated and orders a beer and then he spots her."

Anne knew Sherry didn't do floor dances. The other girls told her that if there wasn't a bottle of champagne on the table and a VIP she's not interested.

Shelly shook her head and laughed again.

"It's a slow night so we egged her on."

"So, what happened?" Anne asked, leaning forward.

Shelly sat straight, squared her shoulders and related the story.

******

As Sherry approached the nervous newcomer, he reached into his striped, button-down shirt and pulled out a large gold crucifix dangling from a thick gold chain. He straightened it on his chest. Sherry just smiled; she knew this boy was not going to be a problem.

"First time here?" she said.

"Yeah, first time," came a giddy reply.

"Sit on your hands. Don't move, just look at me," and she began the dance.

With one foot on the floor and the other on the seat of his chair, she leaned over and whispered in his ear, "How are you tonight?" No answer. She ran her fingers through his slicked-back greasy hair, then down his chest to the belt on his pants, never missing a beat of the music. She leaned back, took off her sequined top and hung it from his ears. Paralyzed, the guy never took his eyes off her. She cupped her breasts in her hands, leaned in again and picked up the gold crucifix between her breasts.

"Catholic?" she asked.

He nodded yes.

"Know Father Riley? He comes in here on Saturday nights after hearing confessions."

A muffled moan came from the customer.

Shelly sat on his lap and started to throw her right leg onto his shoulder but jumped off quickly.

"Holy crap! This dance is over. You owe me a hundred dollars," she told him.

"But you only did one dance; I thought they were three for a hundred."

"Buddy you couldn't handle two more dances, now pay me."

The guy stood up with her sequined top still hanging from his ears, reached into his pocket and handed her two fifty-dollar bills.

"That's it, no tip?"

He handed her another fifty, his hands shaking as she took her sequined top off his ears.

******

Sherry was back in the Dressing Room and walked over to Shelly and Anne.

"That son-of-a-bitch came in his pants, the jerk."

"Obviously, he hasn't been introduced to Mrs. Thumb and her four daughters. Guess you did your job too well," Shelly said and they laughed.

Marco was cleaning the counters and Sherry asked him to get them a drink.

"Hell, I need more than a drink, I need a shower," she said.

By the time she finished her shower Marco was back with their drinks.

"Why are you back here, Shelly? Why aren't you working?"

"I spent three hours with this customer in the VIP. He knew the price was five hundred an hour. I had a feeling I should get my money up front but what idiot goes into the VIP room without money. When I finished he told me he didn't have any money. I called Jerry, he's the head bouncer tonight, thinking he could shake the guy down but this guy just didn't have it, like he said. Imagine that!

"Right now Jerry is driving him to an ATM machine to get the money. He better have fifteen hundred bucks when he slides his card into the machine or he's gonna have a couple of broken ribs. Jerry doesn't fool around. Can't figure out the guys who come in here with no money. Are they stupid? Don't they know the bouncers will take them out back and smash their faces if they don't pay?"

Sherry laughed.

"Lucky guy for picking you. Not so lucky for the creep who came in here and Anita danced for him. He seemed like a nice enough fellow and she spent two hours with him. She didn't get her money up front but he did pay her. He gave her ten one-hundred-dollar bills and he asked for her telephone phone number. Instead, she asked for his business card and said she would call him, never planning to do so. Well, it turned out the bills were counterfeit. Anita let it ride for a couple of days and then called the stupid bastard and he agreed to meet her."

Marco interrupted them and asked if they needed refills. They did.

"They met in one of the casino parking lots and he was excited to see her. She asked him if he knew the money he gave her was counterfeit. The idiot said yes but he would make it up to her. Anita just smiled and invited him over to her Mercedes. He thought they were going for a ride without leaving the parking lot. She opened the passenger door, reached in and pulled out her club. She always carries a club; I prefer a baseball bat. Nonetheless, he was looking around wondering if anybody was watching them when she struck the first blow. She hit him again and again on his arms, legs and back but never touched his face. He was a whimpering mess on the ground with Anita swearing and cussing him out.

"A security guy on his bicycle heard the commotion and rode over to investigate. He asked them for ID. Seems this guy was some big investment banker from L.A. He was asked if he wanted to press charges; needless to say, the answer was no.

"Anita got in her car and drove away. She didn't get her money but oh, the satisfaction of beating the guy made up for it."

Sherry and Shelly were just finishing their second drink when Jerry was back with Shelly's fifteen hundred.

"Thanks, Jerry, you're a real trooper." She handed him two hundred dollars.

They were both ready to go back to work. "C'mon, Shelly, let's go have another kick at the can," Sherry said.

As they headed out, Vivian came through shouting, "Five-O, five-O." Thirty girls came in behind her.

Vice was in the house.

CHAPTER 68

Vivian sat in a corner with her feet up on the counter filing her nails. Other girls were calling their friends and telling them Vice was in the house and not to come to work for at least an hour.

"How long do you think they're gonna stay this time, Viv?" one of the girls asked.

"God only knows. It's the end of the month and those bandits have to get their quota of tickets written up. There won't be any tickets written on the girls tonight for lewd behavior if they behave themselves but those guys will hang around getting their eyes full and copping a feel, believing they are entitled, all part of the job, they tell themselves."

Vivian finished her nails and sauntered over to Anne.

"What do you think of this, Mom? Those cops come in here just lookin' and hopin' for an excuse to haul our asses off to jail. Last month when they were here, Sara was just walking by one of them when a customer reached out and grabbed her ass. She was not amused and tore into the guy and gave him a piece of her mind. The customer shoved her and she fell back against one of the cops, who took full advantage of that move and grabbed her by her breasts. Instead of saying something to the customer, the cop cited her for letting a customer touch her. Some of the girls went to her defense and the cops cited all of them for interfering. Frankie was even cited for telling the girls to spread the word the cops were here. They fined him five hundred, which he paid on the spot and you can bet that five hundred never made it to the coffers. That was a bumper night for the cops, but tonight something is different. There's a lady cop here."

The words were barely out of Vivian's mouth when the purple door opened. She walked tall into the Dressing Room, her hand on her gun, handcuffs hanging from her belt. She looked around the room and spotted Anne. The girls were quiet except for Jamie who had too much to drink. Shaking her booty, with arms straight up in the air, wearing little else than a G-string, she hollered, "Hey, lady, are you here to frisk us? We're not hiding anything, no place to hide a thing." The girls quickly pulled her down into a chair.

The officer had a poster in her hand and as she stepped behind Anne's desk she handed it to her. "The manager said you might be able to identify these girls."

Staring up at her was a photo of two young girls from the Philippines who had started work at the club two months ago. They spoke very little English when they applied for work and Anne asked Tia to interpret for her. With Anne's direction she explained to them the rules and how much they had to pay to work. They had no money but Anne told them they could pay the tip-out when they made it. Tia took them under her wing and watched over them. The girls left work together each night at the same time.

Anne handed the poster back to the officer, who asked, "Do you recognize them?"

Anne said that she did.

"Do you know the last time they worked?"

"Five nights ago."

"Know anyone they might have hung out with?"

"No, they kept to themselves and were picked up each night after work by a man who drove a black Cadillac."

"How do you know that?" the officer asked.

"I watch the girls in the monitor when they leave," Anne explained. "The office should be able to track exactly the last time they worked and the security tapes might show the license plate of the Cadillac."

"Thanks for your help," the officer said.

She turned to leave but stopped and asked, "Aren't you interested in why all the questions about these two girls?"

"I know better than to ask," Anne said with sadness in her voice.

The lady cop came closer to Anne.

"These two girls are sisters and they were found in the desert, shot execution style. We think it was probably a drug deal gone bad."

She handed Anne her card and pinned one of the posters on the bulletin board.

Anne searched the newspapers daily looking for any information on the two sisters who were murdered in the desert. A small article was hidden on the back page. The authorities speculated that it was a drug trade that took a bad turn. It was happening more and more in this fantasy city. People were bombarded on a daily basis with tragic news on the local television station to the point of desensitization.

Murders, armed robberies, children found dead in dumpsters, thousands homeless. The city was becoming a neon jungle.

On her way to work Anne picked up the daily newspaper and on the front page of the second section was a picture of the sisters. A reward of twenty-five thousand dollars was being offered for any information regarding the two girls. The paper was on her desk when Shelly checked in.

"You look very sad tonight, Mom. Is everything okay?"

Anne picked up the newspaper and handed it to Shelly.

"It's heartbreaking," Anne said. "Those two young girls came to America hoping for a better life but their lives were snuffed out before they had a chance. Who would do such a horrible thing?"

"It happens, Mom. A lot of girls are mail-order brides with their own dreams but most are treated like sex slaves when they get here. They don't speak the language, have no idea about our laws or their rights and nowhere to turn when they realize the hell they're in. The lucky ones are put to work in strip clubs; others are turned out to work the streets. Their so-called husbands keep their passports and then they threaten them if they want to leave but we've helped a few.

"Several years ago four girls from the Philippines started work here. God, they were so young. They couldn't speak much English and had no concept of the stripper world. Fortunately for them, Tina was working the night they were hired. They latched onto her when they found out she was from the Philippines. Each night before their shift started Tina would be waiting for them with an armload of children's books, pencils, paper and flash cards. For one hour she would teach them English but she told them not to tell anyone outside the club. She figured if their husbands found out they would be put to work on the streets. Six months later they had a pretty good command of English."

Anne interrupted Shelly, checked in several girls, and then Shelly continued her story.

"Tina noticed they were losing weight and when she asked them about it they told her they were eating just fast food and they really missed their Philippine dishes. Tina brought them dinner every night after that. They worked six nights a week and made pretty good money. Every night Tina took a hundred dollars from each of them to invest. At the end of the year they had close to fifty thousand dollars. That's when Tina really flew into action; the girl was on a mission. She had lots of contacts in the Philippine community and made arrangements for the girls to be picked up at the club and taken to a safe house. Once the girls were safe she called Phil, the lawyer. He knows a lot about immigration law. With his help they got their divorces and, when eligible, received their citizenship.

"The girls continued dancing for another two years, still giving Tina a hundred dollars a night. They took advanced English classes, business and child care courses at the community college. With the money Tina invested for them, they bought a building and opened a daycare center. There is a waiting list to get in.

"Tina realized she loved teaching and enrolled at the university. She didn't have all the credentials to get accepted but they took her anyway; they had to fill their quota of minorities. She graduated top of her class and is now working on her master's degree while teaching school. She is really great at it. Can you imagine if the parents of her students knew she had been a stripper what their reaction would be?

That's Tina's biggest fear — that she will be found out. Any kid who gets her for a teacher is a lucky one indeed.

"So, you see, Mom, it isn't all bad. There are happy stories too."

Anne folded the newspaper and threw it in the trash.

CHAPTER 69

The outside bell was ringing and Anne automatically checked the monitor to see who was there. She took a second look and wasn't surprised to see Natasha and Sylvie standing there looking a little nervous. She buzzed them in.

"Hello, Anne. Do you remember us? We met at Janet's party six months ago. We were so afraid you may have left the club and gone back to practicing law," Natasha said, all in one breath.

"Of course, I remember you, and it's nice to see you but I'm guessing this is not a social call but that you want to work. You must have a very serious reason for doing so," she said with a smile.

"You guessed correctly. We have been preparing for this since we met you. You opened our eyes to the possibility of gaining back our independence and getting out of our marriages. We did a lot of research on this business and have taken Pole Dancing 101 at a studio in Los Angeles. We are pretty good at it and are in the best shape we've been in for a long time. Our husbands know nothing about it."

"Well, let's get the paperwork done and get you to work."

When they were ready to go into the club, Anne introduced them to Shelly and asked her to show them around. Shelly raised an eyebrow and gave Anne an inquiring look that said, "You've got to be kidding, you have friends who want to be strippers? Impossible!"

The three of them went through the purple door together and Anne smiled to herself. Frankie passed them on their way out.

"You look like the cat that just caught the canary," he said. "What are you smiling about and who are those girls who just went into the club with Shelly? I didn't hire them. Are you doing my job now?"

"Just two new girls who started tonight. Their names are Natasha and Sylvie and you must admit they more than meet the criteria to work your shift. Jim told me to hire any girls who were ten's if you weren't around. He doesn't want to lose top-drawer girls waiting for you. You should be careful, Frankie, I could have your job."

"Bullshit to that, but I must say they're lookers alright. I'll go catch up with them and buy them a drink. Maybe they want to see the inside of my office; maybe they want to get to know Frankie a little better."

"You give it your best shot, Frankie, but I wouldn't count on it."

Several hours later Shelly was back.

"What's the story behind Natasha and Sylvie and are they really friends of yours?" she asked.

"We're not close friends, more like acquaintances. I'm not sure why they are dancing but they have their reasons. They are two very bright women with their own agenda."

"They are sharp, and took to the club like a duck to water. For having never danced before, it's amazing how confident they are. I didn't have to tell them very much. They sat at the bar for awhile, taking everything in, and then they put their stilettos to the floor and started making money. They're working together, which is a good idea. Three VIPs, that's fifteen hundred each, not bad, not bad at all."

Three hours later Natasha and Sylvie were back.

"This dancing is a lot of work," Natasha said as she pulled back her long blonde hair and put it in a ponytail then reached down and took off her stilettos. "The public image of this business is so far removed from reality. I've never read anything about the men who frequent strip clubs and all I've ever read about the dancers is how miserable their lives are, how most of them have been sexually abused, molested, beaten and on drugs. Funny, I haven't heard any of that from the dancers we talked to. It may have happened to some girls but that stuff happens in upscale neighborhoods everywhere. Most of the girls we've met tonight are just average Janes making a living on their terms.

"I sure learned a lot tonight," Sylvie said. "Doing a dance is one thing, having to fight off the men with Roman hands and Russian fingers is quite another. Guys who spent nine months trying to get out, now spend the rest of their lives trying to get back in."

"Speaking of trying to get out, we've been wanting to get out of our marriages for quite awhile but didn't know how until we met you, Anne," Natasha said. "The minute you stood up to Sonny Boy — I think that's what you called him — I knew if we followed you we would find a way out. It just took us six months to get here, but we have our plan mapped out."

Sylvie picked up the conversation.

"We are dancing to get the money to complete our university degrees because our husbands won't give us the money. Once we're finished we will file for divorce and that will be a battle, with money being the big issue. We're sure going to need a good lawyer."

"What will you study?" Anne asked.

"Natasha will get her journalism degree and will work at Starlight Publishing, which is owned by my brother, and I will finish my engineering degree."

Natasha put her arm around her friend and said, "Sylvie will have no trouble getting an engineering position; she is brilliant."

"Do you see Janet often?" they asked.

Anne chuckled. "Don't worry about me saying anything to Janet. Your plans are safe with me."

"It's getting late. Our husbands are gambling and they think we're at a show. Fortunately, they lose track of time when playing the tables. We'll be back tomorrow night."

CHAPTER 70

When they left, Marco came to Anne and just nodded his head toward a dancer on the other side of the Dressing Room.

She was sitting alone on the six-foot-long varnished bench staring into the makeup mirror but not really seeing her reflection. Her waist-length hair in braids tied with red ribbons lay lifeless on her perfect back. Her shoulders were shaking and the tears she shed formed a pool on the counter; her index finger making circles in the pool of tears.

Anne walked over and sat down. She put her arm around the ninety-pound dancer who went by the name of Lucky. She leaned her head on Anne's shoulder and said, in broken English, "My husband isn't nice to me. He will beat me again tonight because I haven't made enough money. I'm so tired, I just want to sleep until it all goes away."

She leaned in closer to Anne.

"I didn't like him but my father said I would get used to him. He paid five hundred dollars for me because I was a virgin and my family needed the money he promised to send them every month, but he never kept his promise."

"A couple of months ago I found out I was pregnant and I was so happy because I would have someone to love but he made me get an abortion. He said we couldn't afford a baby and that was not why he married me. We needed money, not a baby. I want to run away but have nowhere to go."

Shelly had been sitting nearby and overheard the conversation. She left the Dressing Room in search of Tia.

"I feel guilty sometimes because I wouldn't be an American if I hadn't married him. That was a happy day for me when I became a citizen and held my passport, but my husband took it away and locked it up. He told me it didn't matter that I was an American, he could send me back to Thailand any time he wanted."

She put her fragile arms around Anne.

"I have to go back to work, it's getting late and he will be here at three o'clock to get me. I haven't made enough money and he will beat me again. I am so afraid of him."

"Lucky, you are not alone and there are people who can help you," Anne said.

Shelly came through the purple door and she held it open for Lucky as Anne was walking back to her desk.

"I overheard your conversation with Lucky and I have spoken to Tia. She will alert her people that Lucky needs help and get her to a safe house tonight, and I also called Phil, who will take care of things from his end. Someone will be here within the hour to get Lucky."

Tia came into the Dressing Room with her arm around Lucky, who was crying and smiling at the same time. They changed into street clothes with Tia watching over Lucky like a mother hen protecting her chicks. "If only she would protect herself in the same way," Anne thought.

The doorbell rang and Tia looked into the monitor and recognized the angel that would take Lucky to safety.

Anne hugged Lucky, who seemed frozen with fear. Anne didn't know if it was fear of the unknown or fear of her husband's reaction. She watched the monitor as the car carrying Tia and Lucky left the parking lot. She wondered where they were going. The girls shared everything with her but when it came to the business of hiding the girls who needed help she was told nothing and she knew Tia appreciated the fact that she never asked.

She was with her own thoughts and didn't realize Frankie was standing at her desk staring at her. "What are you up to?" he asked. "You look like you have something heavy on your mind."

"I could tell you, Frankie, but I doubt you would understand."

"Give it a try," he answered, laughing.

Anne told him what had transpired and said she thought Lucky's husband would go a little crazy when he came to pick her up and found she was gone.

"I know her husband," he said and Anne could feel the anger building in him. "He's a son-of-a-bitch, drives a cab, and makes a ton of money and the bastard beats up on that little woman. When he shows up, call me immediately and I'll go outside and meet him and tell him his wife isn't here. Are you sure she's okay? Where did she go, who took her?"

"I don't have any details, Frankie, but I will call you when he shows up."

As he was walking out, he turned and said, "You're a real doll for helping the girls."

Anne looked up. "Wrong again, Frankie; a doll is an empty-headed plaything."

He just shook his head and left, knowing there was no way he could win.

At 2:55 am, Lucky's husband rang the bell and said into the intercom that he was here to pick up his wife and to tell her to make it snappy, he was in a hurry.

Anne called Frankie on her radio but he didn't answer. The husband was back hollering into the intercom, demanding Lucky, and said he would take the door down and come in and get her himself.

Anne called Frankie again and told him the husband was going to kick in the door. He laughed. "I'm on my way." He came into the Dressing Room with Bill and Dan, two of the toughest bouncers. They were all grinning.

"Don't worry, Mom, the Marines are here," they shouted and headed out the door.

Anne couldn't hear what they were saying but did see the son-of-a-bitch tried to take down Frankie and the bouncers. Big mistake. The three guys were on him like a fox on a rabbit and when they came up for air it wasn't a pretty sight. It was over in seconds.

They came back inside with their chests all puffed up.

"He won't give Lucky any more problems. Told him if he bothered her we would break his kneecaps next time and he wasn't to come on the property, which means he will lose a lot of money. You know these cabbies get twenty dollars for every customer they bring here and he would bring at least forty a night. I hope Lucky comes back to work. I'll protect her."

Anne gave him a disgusted look. "Sure Frankie, you're all about protecting the girls."

A month later Lucky came back to work and told Anne she had a new passport and divorce papers. "That Mr. Phil is a very smart lawyer. I really am Lucky now."

Another one saved.

CHAPTER 71

Anne spent several hours in a local bookstore on her day off and was drawn to a table displaying "How-to Books" — how to start a diet, an exercise program, to cook and how to write. She picked up a book on Creative Writing, another on Creating Characters and thumbed through them. Tucking them under her arm she picked up a Dictionary for Writers, a thesaurus, and a gift bag and headed for the cashier. Her next stop was the grocery store and then she could go home and have a relaxing evening.

Fortunately the store wasn't too busy and she had a basketful of nutritious food for the girls in no time, as well as several pads of paper, pens and pencils that she picked up in the stationery aisle. She headed for the cashier when a shopper accidentally bumped into her cart. It was Shelly and she was apologetic as she hugged Anne. "What a surprise running into you, literally."

Anne laughed. "I've just finished my shopping; have you finished? Perhaps we could go for a coffee or glass of wine?"

"Sounds good to me, I could use a glass of wine right now. Let's meet at The Bistro, it's just a block from here."

They arrived at the Bistro within seconds of each other and were seated at an outdoor table. It was early evening, the sun was starting its descent and there was a balmy breeze.

They each ordered a glass of Chardonnay and shared an appetizer of steamed artichokes with drawn butter.

Anne made a toast to inner peace as she reached for the gift bag that was leaning up against her chair and handed it to Shelly.

"This is for you," she said.

Shelly graciously accepted the gift bag. One by one she laid the books on the table. She picked up the Creative Writing Book and held it to her heart. "I am at a loss for words, Anne. No one has ever taken an interest in me or even taken the time to listen. I've felt so alone for a long time and here you are offering this wonderful gift. You barely know me. I am beyond words of thanks."

"You don't ever give up on your dreams, Shelly. You have a passion for writing and that will always be with you."

"What could I possibly write about? I have been nothing but a stripper my entire life."

"That in itself would interest people. In fact, most people are fascinated with the business. I can attest to that. When I told my family and friends that I was going to work in a gentlemen's club as a House Mom, you would never have believed the reaction. Most were very shocked, but now they all want to hear about my girls. Write what you know about. Nobody knows this business as well as you."

"Every day when you wake up, sit with your morning coffee and write. You might also consider taking a writing course at the community college. Now, let's order another glass of wine and have a toast to happy endings."

CHAPTER 72

When Ashley signed in for the night shift she had a big smile on her face and without saying a word plunked her left hand down on Anne's desk. On the third finger was a very impressive, beautiful marquise-cut diamond ring with two shoulder baguettes.

"Guess what, Mom? I'm getting married and I want you to be the mother of the bride."

Anne looked at Ashley and thought, "Oh, no, not again."

Ashley was all smiles as she told Anne of her plans. The wedding would take place at the Diamond Gardens and a magnificent reception would follow with great music and dancing. It was a very exclusive and expensive place but her father was paying for everything and had given her a budget of seventy thousand dollars. He wanted the best for his little girl.

She had found the perfect dress and it was only five thousand dollars. Made of imported silk, it was covered in pearls and crystals and had a twenty-five-foot train. A shoulder-length veil with pearls and crystals would adorn her head. She would have six attendants, live music plus a DJ. The video people were hired as well as a photographer. The limousines were hired, tuxedos rented.

"It will be a black tie affair and the classiest wedding ever that no one will forget for a long, long time," Ashley beamed.

Anne took a breath and wondered about the groom. It was all about the ring, the dress and the party. His name wasn't even mentioned.

"Who's the lucky fellow?" Anne asked.

"Oh, I almost forgot!" Ashley giggled. "You will love him, Mom. He works as a bartender at a nightclub in a casino on the Strip. He does okay but doesn't make as much money as me, but we'll get by."

Anne remembered Ashley telling her she made two hundred thousand dollars last year.

"I'm buying him a red Beamer for a wedding gift. He would probably like a truck but he's getting a car, just in case. I hope he likes it.

"The reason I want you to be my mother of the bride," Ashley continued, "is because I don't have a mother. She abandoned me when I was two years old and Dad raised me on his own. We've never heard from her and even if we did I wouldn't want her at my wedding. Dad said she was a tramp and ran off with some guy in a red Mustang. It really tore him up. He did a good job raising me, always wanted me to go to college but when I turned twenty-one years old I went into stripping. I was born and raised in this city and you learn real fast where the money is. Dad has always hung out at strip cubs so when I told him I wanted to strip he hooked me up with a friend of his who owned a club. I danced there for a while but always wanted to work here. Dad's here a lot and the girls love him; he drops a lot of money on them. The next time he's here, I'll introduce you to him."

Six other girls who were listening to Ashley's conversation came over to get a look at the ring.

"Wow, that's quite a rock. How many carats?" one of them asked.

"As a matter of fact, it is two carats, a perfect stone," Ashley said. "I just asked Mom to be the mother of the bride, but she hasn't said yes yet."

In a single chorus they said, "You've got to, Mom, you would be perfect. If you do, we'll make sure you have a good time. You *are* going to invite all of us, aren't you, Ashley?"

Ashley ignored the question.

"We're being married on a Monday night, Mom, your night off, so you can come."

Anne wasn't too sure about this but she reluctantly gave in. There was much whooping and hollering in the Dressing Room and Ashley kept talking to the girls about the wedding as they got ready for work.

Amid it all, Frankie came in wanting to know what all the noise was about.

"Ashley's getting married and Mom is going to be the mother of the bride," the girls said. "This is so exciting!"

Frankie leaned on Anne's desk and gave her a leer.

"So, mother of the bride, is it? Well, it seems to me you're going to need an escort and I'll volunteer. You couldn't get a better man for the job. Whadda you say? Is it a date?"

Anne shook her head and laughed, "Fat chance, Frankie, fat chance."

Over the next few weeks, Anne and Ashley went over the details of the wedding from planning the menu to the budget.

"Dad thinks ten thousand dollars should cover the dinner and another fifteen thousand should cover the bar; do you think that will be enough?"

"That will be plenty," Anne said and thought how their priorities were out of sync: a bigger budget for the bar than for the dinner.

Time flew by and the big day arrived.

She had chosen a V-neck, long sapphire blue gown with cap sleeves. From her jewelry box she selected a diamond and sapphire pendant set in platinum with matching stud earrings that Philip had given her for Christmas many years before.

She arrived at the Diamond Gardens and pulled up to Valet where a young man in a crisp, white tuxedo shirt and black bow tie offered his hand to her as she stepped from the car.

"Welcome to the Bowman wedding," he said, "and may I have your name?"

"I'm Anne Baxter, a guest of the bride's."

He looked down the guest list.

"Oh, a very special guest, you are the mother of the bride. Please come this way."

He escorted her to another young man who was dressed in a black tuxedo with a name tag that read "Trevor, Captain's Assistant," who led Anne into the gardens where another young man was waiting with a tray of champagne in crystal flutes. He handed her a flute and she thanked the two young men as they left.

It seemed she was the first to arrive as she strolled across the marble terrace sipping her champagne. Her eyes swept across the superb expanse of freshly cut grass and the scent blended with hundreds of flowers in granite containers. The sun poured down like butterscotch on a gazebo where the bride and groom would take their vows. It was wrapped in a gauzy fabric that shifted in the breeze.

A couple with a teenage girl was sitting on a bench close by. Anne walked over to them and introduced herself and said she was a guest of the bride and commented on the beautiful surroundings.

"We're the groom's parents and this is his sister. Yes, it is nice here, at least she did that right, but we know how she makes her money and that her father is paying for this extravaganza. We're not paying for anything but we weren't asked to help. Imagine, a stripper in a place like this; what is this world coming to? Our son could have done so much better. Why he picked her is beyond belief; marrying a stripper, of all things. By the way, how do you know the bride? You certainly don't look or talk like someone she would know, you're much too classy."

Anne cleared her throat and smiled, "I work in the same strip club as the bride." And she turned and slowly walked away.

The guests were milling around outside and there was excitement in the air. Trevor, the captain's assistant, asked them to take their seats and he sought out Anne and escorted her to her place on the bride's side of the white carpet.

The groom and his groomsmen were standing in place as the five bridesmaids made their way down to the gazebo followed by Ashley on her father's arm.

No one could deny she was a vision in her designer gown. Her father lifted her veil and kissed her on the cheek as he handed her over to his future son-in-law and sat down next to Anne. Anne couldn't believe her eyes; to her horror, Ashley was chewing gum. The pastor began by welcoming the guests and saying how wonderful it was that Ashley and Warren would be united in matrimony.

The vows were taken, rings exchanged and the minister said to the groom, "You may now kiss your bride."

Warren grabbed Ashley and dipped her over. She lost her balance and the gum popped out of her mouth and stuck to her veil but Warren held on and gave his bride a long wet kiss. He picked her up and planted her firmly on her feet. Her expression was not one of delight, but when the pastor said, "I now give you Mr. & Mrs. Bowman," she managed a smile.

The photographer whisked the bride and groom away to take photographs and the music started up. Anne felt a touch on her elbow and turned. It was Laura, one of the bridesmaids, who asked her to come quickly and get the gum off Ashley's veil. Anne took a piece of ice from a nearby ice bucket and went to the bride and removed the gum.

"Thanks, Mom. I could just kill Warren for dipping me like that; he wrecked my veil and hair. He's an idiot."

Shortly after, the captain announced that dinner was served and the guests should please take their seats. He came to Anne and said he would escort her to her place at the family table. When she sat down, she saw a small plaque on a gold stand at her place setting with the words, "A Mother's Love Is Forever." Sitting to her right was Bert, the bride's father, who was quite intoxicated; to her left was the bride's sister, Mindy, who had a cane by her side. Apparently she sprained her ankle two days before the wedding and couldn't be in the wedding party. The groom's parents were nowhere to be seen.

The dining room was decked out in pink and white flowers, beautiful white linen covered the table tops set with sterling silver flatware, crystal stemware stood at attention and a centerpiece of baby pink roses completed the detail. Nothing was missed. Two servers were in attendance at each table and dinner was served without a flaw. Glasses were raised in many toasts to the bride and groom and speeches made and a lot of laughter filled the room.

The tables were cleared after dinner and the band started playing. Soon the dance floor filled up quickly with young people gyrating across the floor to terrible music.

Anne was now alone with Bert and Ashley's sister. With slurred speech, Bert told Anne that the Bank of Dad was now closed. The wedding had cost him more than he thought it would and, really, how long did she think this marriage would last?" Warren's family hated Ashley; they didn't think she was good enough for their precious son.

He took a long drink from his highball glass.

"Hell, he's nothing but a bartender. Ashley makes more money than he does. Even the ring he gave her, he bought on time, and Ashley had to pay off the balance a few days before the wedding. He's nothing special," Bert said as he lifted a bottle of Scotch and poured himself another drink.

A bridesmaid came rushing over and said there was a fight going on in the ladies room and she needed help. She went on to explain that she was there doing her business when the groom's mother and sister came in. "They were really bashing Ashley, saying all sorts of mean things about her, like she was nothing but a fucking stripper and how much they hated her and they're really pissed off that they were seated at the back of the room, almost into the fucking kitchen. Ashley walked into this and caught the end of their conversation. She came back at them with words of her own and it wasn't looking pretty."

Mindy jumped up, grabbed her cane and limped toward the ladies room. "You'd better do something, Dad, and fast. A fight is coming down," she said over her shoulder.

"Are their shoes off?" he said laughing. "Let them tear each other apart. I don't care. I need another drink. You go, Anne, and see if you can calm things down. It seems to me you're the only one here with any brains."

Anne left the table and followed Laura and Mindy to the ladies room. She opened the door to total chaos. Ashley and four of her friends had the groom's mother and sister up against the wall, shouting that no one talked about Ashley like that. Mindy made her way to the terrified women, swirling her cane through the air.

Anne got to Ashley and managed to get her out of the room.

"I want those fuckin' bastards off this property right now," Ashley demanded.

Trevor was outside the door with total bewilderment in his eyes. "Nothing like this has ever happened at the Diamond Gardens before," he said as two security guards were approaching.

Anne went back into the ladies room just in time to grab Mindy's spinning cane out of her hand. Without the cane Mindy lost her balance and fell onto the leather sofa but managed to pick herself up and went for the mother-in-law again.

Anne stepped between them and held out her hands to the mother-in-law, almost pleading, "Perhaps it is better that you leave. Security is outside and Ashley wants you off the property."

To Anne's surprise, she agreed, saying that she didn't want anything more to do with this "white trailer trash." Anne started to open the door when Mindy came from behind and shoved the mother-in-law. She, in turn, punched Mindy in the face. Anne grabbed the mother-in-law and her daughter and got them out of the room.

The captain and his assistants were lined up outside the door and their faces told all that they were thinking.

"It's going to be okay," Anne said. "Could you please bring their car to the side door?"

"It's already there," said the captain, "and the husband is at the wheel ready to take off."

Unbeknownst to Anne, one of the bridesmaids had found Ashley and told her the mother-in-law punched Mindy in the face. All hell broke loose.

As the mother-in-law was getting into the car she saw Ashley running toward the car with her twenty-five-foot train flying through the air. She moved quickly and locked the door but wasn't fast enough in rolling up the window. Ashley's fist connected with her nose and the blood faucet was turned on. She pulled back her fist to hit her again but the window had been put up. Ashley hit the window and let out a scream. The car took off, leaving her with an injured hand. Everyone rushed to her, cursing the mother-in-law. Warren was crying and blubbering about how his wife had just beaten up his mother.

The video guy was having a field day capturing the whole thing on tape.

"Hurry, Mom, Ashley needs you. Her hand is swelling up and looks weird," shouted a bridesmaid.

"I think your hand may be broken, Ashley," Anne told her. "We have to take you to emergency now."

"I'm not going anywhere. I have to cut my wedding cake and we are going to the Bahamas on our honeymoon," she cried as the waterproof mascara started running down her face. "Go get Warren and tell him to find Josh. He's a paramedic and will know how to fix this."

Bleary-eyed Josh appeared holding a bottle of beer. After looking at Ashley's hand he felt it was just fractured. He said he could make a splint with a couple of wooden spoons and some duct tape. Two wooden spoons were brought from the kitchen along with the roll of needed tape. He secured her hand, taped it to the spoons and gave her a Vicodin, which he pulled from his back pocket. They all went into the reception to cut the cake. The other guests, quite oblivious to the fight, were into the fountain of champagne and kicking up their heels on the dance floor.

Ashley wrapped a white linen napkin over her taped-up hand and, with a big smile, cut the cake. She picked up a big piece and fed it to Warren, spreading it all over his face. Anne thought he was going to cry again.

The DJ announced the bride and groom would have their first dance as man and wife. Anne walked back to her table to gather up her things. Bert was passed out, sprawled across the table holding onto his drink.

There was a well-dressed, petite blonde woman standing by Anne's seat looking at the little plaque. "I know who you are, but you don't know me," she said. "I am Ashley's mother, Margaret, and I can only imagine the story she has told you. You have met her father," she glanced over at her ex-husband, "and I'm sure you have formed your own opinion of him. We were divorced almost ten years ago when Ashley was turning sixteen and Mindy twelve. He convinced Ashley to stay with him and if she did he would buy her a new car; Mindy came to live with me. I tried to keep a relationship with Ashley but Bert made it difficult, and I was devastated when she started to strip. She was smart in school and I had hopes she would go to university."

"When Mindy sprained her ankle she cried that she wouldn't be able to be Ashley's bridesmaid and that's how I learned my daughter was getting married. My heart sank when Mindy told me I wasn't invited; it was a very painful thing to hear. Although I wasn't invited, I couldn't stay away."

Bert started to groan and Ashley's mother shook Anne's hand and turned to leave.

"I think you're forgetting something, Margaret. This belongs to you." She handed her the little plaque, "A Mother's Love Is Forever."

Anne picked up her belongings and walked to the door. She looked over her shoulder and took in the room. The candles were burning down, the music played on and the bride and groom were staring into each other's eyes. Picture perfect, or so it seemed, but things, as we all know, are rarely what they seem.

How long did the marriage last? About as long as the honeymoon.

Ashley's mother was right when she said her daughter was smart; the Beamer she bought Warren as a wedding gift was in her name and the receipt for the marquise-cut diamond was also in her name. Ashley was right when she said it would be a wedding no one would ever forget for a long, long time.

As Anne waited for her car she remembered what her grand-mother had always said, "You can have class without money but money can't buy you class. It is something you are taught."

CHAPTER 73

The wedding was the topic of conversation for days and, after an exhausting Friday night with Frankie, Anne was glad to be home.

She laid her purse down on the hall table when she came in the door and noticed the message light was blinking on her answering machine. She pressed the answer button.

"Aunt Anne, its John. Scott and I are coming to Vegas tomorrow to attend a convention and hope you have time to see us. We would like to visit the Tiger Club. Perhaps we can have dinner and go there after. I'll call as soon as we get checked in."

Anne changed into comfy clothes, poured herself a glass of wine and went out to the patio. Dawn would be breaking soon as she thought about her nephew. He and Scott were friends from elementary school through to graduation from medical school. They opened a practice together, which thrived from the beginning. Both were now thirty-five years old and considered to be the most eligible bachelors in town, although John had reconnected with his high school sweetheart and there would probably be a wedding in the near future. She looked forward to seeing them.

The sun was up as Anne put her wine glass in the dishwasher and went to bed feeling much better than when she came home. Remarkable, really, how a thirty-second phone message from someone you love can shift you from feeling down to lifting you up.

CHAPTER 74

Before leaving to meet her nephew and Scott for dinner, Anne called the club and spoke to Donny, the manager on duty, and told him her nephew and his friend would be coming to the club and to please give them the VIP treatment. He assured her he would take care of them.

At dinner John brought Anne up to date on the news from home, with the biggest news being that he planned to ask Judy Bradshaw to marry him. "I hope you will attend the wedding, Aunt Anne, you haven't been home for a long time."

They drove to the club after dinner and, when Anne pulled into Valet, Donny was waiting for them. After introductions he told Anne he would look after "the boys" although he didn't think they would have any trouble taking care of themselves; they were six foot two and very fit. He then escorted Anne to the Dressing Room.

An hour later Donny told Anne his shift was ending and Frankie was now on the floor. He had met John and Scott and bought them a drink and was now pumping them for information about her.

"What are you laughing about, Mom?" Marilyn asked as she was checking in.

"Oh, my nephew and his business partner are here tonight and Frankie is trying to get information from them about me."

"Frankie says you confuse him. When I go out on the floor I'll look for your nephew and introduce myself."

Several girls came up to Anne and asked, "Is it true that's your nephew and his friend out in the club? Frankie says so but we don't believe anything he says. They are really gorgeous and they're wearing really expensive suits."

"What do they do for a living?" Veronica asked.

"They are doctors, so behave yourselves and don't take advantage of them," Anne said.

"Hmm... sounds like the entire package. I will definitely introduce myself," Marilyn said.

It was busy and Anne had little time to think about her nephew and Scott until Jeremy came to see her. "I just want you to know that Marilyn is sitting with Scott and he is spending a lot of money on her. They've been talking most of the time but she does a dance for him every now and then. John, on the other hand, isn't really interested in the girls, says he is planning on marrying his high school sweetheart, and I get the impression he wants to leave. He's standing outside the Dressing Room door so maybe you want to say goodbye to him.

Anne found her nephew leaning up against the wall looking very bored. "Do you want to leave now, John? If you can wait another half hour I will be getting off shift and we can go for something to eat. What about Scott, is he ready to leave?"

"I don't know about Scott, he seems pretty taken with Marilyn. She just told him her shift is just about over and she would be checking out. Perhaps she could come with us."

"No, that's not a good idea, and I rather doubt Marilyn would want to come."

"I wouldn't say that, Aunt Anne, she seems pretty taken with him."

"Jeremy will let you know when I leave and I will meet you at the front door. I can guarantee Scott will be with you, and alone."

Twenty minutes later Marilyn was checking out.

"Scott is really adorable, Mom. I like him but I am feeling a little guilty because he has spent a lot of money on me. Tonight he gave me two thousand dollars. If you didn't know him I wouldn't give a damn, but I don't want you to think I'm taking advantage of him. I've only danced a couple of times for him but we have talked about everything under the sun."

"Marilyn, you're just doing your job and if he enjoys your company and wanted all your time tonight, then so be it. He's a smart man; he knows what he's doing."

Anne understood why Scott would be attracted to Marilyn. She was a beautiful girl from Japan who came to the States to study business at the university six years ago and, like a lot of university graduates who danced their way through school, she came back to dancing because of the money.

Anne radioed Jeremy that she was leaving and drove to the front door where John and Scott were waiting. There was much handshaking going on between the men and the staff with promises to return. They got into Anne's car and decided to go to her place rather than a restaurant.

While Anne whipped together an omelette, Scott couldn't stop talking about Marilyn. He was falling hard for her and was positive she was falling for him. They just had one more night in Vegas and he didn't know when he would get back but she could visit him and they could call each other.

"I have never met anyone like her. She is so beautiful and educated. Did you know she has her master's in business? She said she tried working in the real world but couldn't adapt to the regular hours and so many rules, plus she was only making eighty thousand dollars a year; she does triple that dancing and she works her own hours. Do you believe in love at first sight, Anne?"

Anne took a breath and remembered how she had fallen in love with Philip at first sight. "It can happen, Scott, and sometimes it works and sometimes it doesn't; in your case, I don't think it will. Be careful, I don't want to see you hurt."

"I don't know why you would say that. She told me she would come and visit me."

Anne poured coffee and sat down.

"Did she also tell you she is married with two small children? She dances at night while her husband watches the children and studies for his law degree. The money Marilyn makes dancing is paying for his education. When he graduates she will stop dancing and will pursue a business career. She hates dancing but it is fast, easy money."

"I can't believe that," Scott said.

John had been listening silently to the conversation and spoke up. "Scott, if Christ came down off the cross and told you what Aunt Anne just told you, you wouldn't believe Him either. Accept it, ol' boy.

And now we have to get going. Let's skip the convention and get a flight out of here today."

John turned to Anne and said, "Tell me, Aunt Anne, is it just crazies who come to this city or does this city make you crazy?"

"A little of both, John."

They said their goodbyes and Anne promised to come home for the wedding.

CHAPTER 75

A dozen red roses in a crystal vase were on Anne's desk with an engraved envelope bearing her name. She put the envelope aside and when she was satisfied everything was in place for her last shift, she opened it and pulled out an engraved invitation.

Your presence is requested

At a Farewell Celebration

For Anne Baxter

Our House Mom

At the Sunset Country Club

Saturday, February 28th

Cocktails 7:00 pm • Dinner 8:00 pm

Followed by an evening of dancing

Formal attire • RSVP

The girls stood silently and watched as she reached for a tissue and dried her eyes.

"Don't cry, Mom. Since you told us you are leaving, we've shed enough tears to turn the desert into an ocean."

Anne recalled their reaction when she told them two weeks ago that she would be retiring. It was a hard decision to make. The eight years she had been their House Mom had been fulfilling, but it was now time to go home.

Frankie came into the Dressing Room and told everyone to get back to work and that there would be a new House Mom, and probably a better one. The girls ignored him but Anne gave them the Mom look and they left.

He picked up the invitation, looked it over and said the Sunset Country Club was a classy joint, maybe too classy for Anne and her girls but not for him because he was a member.

"Oh, Frankie, don't worry, I'll make sure the girls and I behave ourselves, I promise we won't embarrass you."

"I know you're just being smart again, Anne," he said.

CHAPTER 76

Anne dressed for the gala celebration and caressed her beautiful floor-length gown of chiffon in a deep shade of yellow with an overlay of a paler shade of yellow Belgian lace; a scalloped hemline moved elegantly when she walked. It was designed and made for her by Lila and her partner Isabella, two former dancers who danced their way through Fashion Design School.

When she went for the final fitting and to make payment, they made it very clear there would be no charge. "This is our gift to you, which barely makes up for the gift you gave us with all your support while we were going through school. We don't think we would have made it without you."

A limousine had been ordered and it arrived promptly at 6:30 pm. On the drive to the country club, Anne wondered what the evening would bring, who would be there and what they were planning. She hoped there would be no surprises. "I don't like surprises," she said to herself.

Shelly was waiting when the limousine pulled up to the club. The driver opened the door and Shelly reached in and took Anne's hand. "I'm your lady-in-waiting tonight, Anne, and I will be at your beck and call for anything that you may need as you have been there for me during the past eight years. I am going to make sure you have an evening you will never forget.

Over two hundred girls with their dates were waiting when they entered the ballroom. They applauded and welcomed her, all of them dressed to the nines. What a spectacular sight.

Hidden behind them was Frankie. He stepped forward wearing a tuxedo, holding an orchid corsage.

"This is for you," he said as he took a step closer and kissed her on the cheek.

"Frankie, you look dashing, and is that a tear I see in your eye?" His hard fist wiped the tear away and he handed her the corsage.

"Okay, enough of this, let's get this party going," he said. "I don't have all night and I'm missing work and God only knows how much this little shindig is costing me."

"Leave it to Frankie, Anne," Shelly said. "He told us to keep it a secret that he is picking up the entire tab for the evening but he just had to let you know. Perhaps it's his way of saying that he will miss you, too."

Frankie was the master of ceremonies for the night and he stood at the podium tapping the microphone, telling everyone to take their seats because dinner was being served.

"If anyone has something to say to Anne you can say it during dinner. Just come up here and speak." Everyone clapped, which Frankie expected.

There were many toasts during dinner and the girls spoke of funny things that happened over the years. The funniest, of course, was the water pipes coming down. Frankie, even several years later, could find no humor in that incident.

Dana flew in from New York, now a thirty-something real estate tycoon. Two years ago she called Anne to tell her she was moving to the Big Apple. "New York is the place to be to really make it big but I'll be back and forth, Mom, and I'll always stay in touch with you." Anne was very proud of her.

Natasha and Sylvie came in from California and had hung up their stilettos when they met their goal of finishing their university degrees. They told Anne they did get their divorces and full custody of their children. Shelly had introduced them to an amazing lawyer who cleaned their former husband's clocks. It was a battle, but he did it.

Natasha thanked Anne for calling her when Shelly finished her first novel. "It was the first novel I published and she is now working on a sequel. We are negotiating with several producers in L.A. to flip it into a movie." Shelly, too, had hung up her stilettos and would never have to worry about money again.

"There are many times we sit with a glass of wine and remember you and wonder if you hadn't been at Janet's party and taken the time to talk to Natasha, where we would be today. We will never forget you," Sylvie said.

The tables were cleared and Frankie announced the dancing and real partying would begin.

Anne excused herself and went to the ladies lounge to freshen up. She stood before the mirror counting her blessings; she had so much to be thankful for, but felt something was missing in her life. She was surrounded by people who loved her but she felt alone.

When she returned to the party, Frankie was waiting for her outside the ladies lounge but Anne's attention was drawn to Shelly and a dozen or more girls at the front door hugging a strange man, and she wondered who he might be. Frankie touched her on the shoulder and brought her back into the moment.

"Is your dance card full or did you leave a space for me?" he said as he took her arm and led her to the dance floor. He twirled her around the floor with ease and style and insisted on a second dance but Shelly interrupted them and said she had someone she wanted Anne to meet.

He stood with his back to her but there was no need for him to turn around. She would recognize the curve of his back anywhere. He turned slowly, with his familiar smile, and looked directly at her. Time stood still.

Shelly was confused. "Do you know each other?" she asked.

Philip took Anne's hand and his touch awakened her heart strings as that touch had done so many years ago.

He guided her onto the dance floor and held her tight. Bending down, he whispered, "I'll never let you go again." She leaned into his chest and could feel tears of joy. She was home, never to be alone again.

It was a perfect farewell celebration with the promise of a new tomorrow, and not one seven-inch stiletto flew over Anne's head.

29173814R00177

Made in the USA
Charleston, SC
04 May 2014